Country Store
Counter Jars
and Tins

Steve Batson

77 Lower Valley Road, Atglen, PA 19310

Disclaimer

This book is not authorized by any of the companies mentioned. The author makes no claim to the ownership of any of the copyrights, names, or trademarks used by any company mentioned or illustrated in this book. Every effort has been made to acknowledge proper ownership and the sole purpose of this book is to preserve the history of these American icons.

The prices quoted in this book are generated from a variety of sources. They are not absolute and the author makes no guarantee of their accuracy. Prices vary due to geography and condition. These prices are based on averaging in the deep South and certainly do not reflect isolated sales trends or how one individual may view value when pricing for a shop or show. Pricing is a subjective art relative to condition and desire. Buy at your own risk ... and join the parade of fools that I lead.

Why everyone needs the book?

This book is a fine primer not only for collectors of jars and tins, but also anyone who has an interest in any of the systems of distribution associated with cookies, candy, and snack foods. This book also serves to establish common advertising and distribution trends and the dates associated with those trends. It is a thorough look at current costs and evaluation of this type of country store antique. An overlooked corner of the world of county store antiques for many years, this guide covers not only Nabisco™, Lance™, Tom's™, Bunte™, and Planter's™, but also over seventy-five other companies. Mention is also made of over two hundred companies that profoundly affected every type of snack food from chewing gum to cookies. The book explores the origins of these companies and provides information about general marketing trends and specific brands that will allow the reader to date, price, and access a wide range of items. The applications extend far beyond the scope of jars and tins, but in that area of collecting, this book will become a prime source for every collector.

Published by Schiffer Publishing Ltd.
77 Lower Valley Road
Atglen, PA 19310
(610) 593-1777
fax (610) 593-2002
Please write for a free catalog.
This book may be purchased
from the publisher.
Please include $2.95 for shipping.
Try your bookstore first.

We are interested in hearing from authors
with book ideas on related subjects.

Table Of Contents

Acknowledgments

Knowledge is never unique or original, it is only borrowed from others. If errors are present, they are mine. I have attempted to acknowledge sources of information and encouragement. Some have been ignored or forgotten, but they were not unappreciated.

Richard Sawyer did yeoman's work with the photography. If he had not been willing to spend time taking most of these photos, I could not have finished this work as you see it. I also suspect it would never have been published.... and he did it for nothing but friendship.

Leon Helms, Hall Lance, Mark Woodson, Lawrence Knighton, and Ann S. Yarborough and family all made very tangible contributions to this work, as did the following, whom I wish to acknowledge.

There are many to thank, my parents, wife, and family, claimed and unclaimed, known and unknown, and my daughters, God's great gift to fat bald-headed aging men. Lyla and Voncie, the premiere prototypes of all that should be, and can be, if we treat each other well and all that is new, bright, and shiny, respectively: love if not eternal runs deep and strong. Fred, Rachel, Camille, (how do you spell that?) Emmett, Ember, and Holly also spent many hours being bored to death and expressing support and interest. Mr. Serff of Tom's™ and Jim Arnold of Moore's offered assistance and support at precisely the time when I felt this was not only stupid but hopeless. Again, Lawrence Knighton who is the embodiment of all that was lost and all that was saved in the South. He remains one of the two sharpest traders I have ever known and a man I admire greatly.

Also Gary and Sister and the dream that was and is NASCAR and small town business, to Dr. G., Greenville Tec., and second chances, Dan, Howell, Buddy, and all the dusty Philos, and the Clan Thompson, to Martha and Mac as well as Bruce Cazel in Wisconsin, also Peter Schiffer for his faith, Jeff Snyder for his work and knowledge and that lovely lady who answers the telephone at Schiffer Publishing, and finally, to my father, Mann Batson, around whom all that is wise revolves and to whom many who are wise defer. To all the readers, whether critics or supporters, enemies or friends, I hope this is a beginning, not an end; and to all the Batsons that ever were or ever shall be, whether they know or even care that they are Batsons or not, I remain, respectfully and gratefully yours,

Steve

I would hope to be able to follow this text with other books on specific companies: Lance™, Tom's™, Gordon's™, Bunte™, Nabisco™, and others which lend themselves to a deeper study. I cannot do this without your help. If you have historical data or unusual items, please let me know.

This is your book. Please tell me what I don't know and what you do. Hopefully, more books can follow.

Steve Batson
10 Batson Lane
Travelers Rest, S.C. 29690
(864) 834-3327

Introduction

Packaging History

In this era of sterile packaging and ageless, prepackaged, individually sealed products the issues of freshness and contamination are dead ones. This was not always the case. Until recently, candy, cookies, potato chips, and other products were shipped to stores or distributors in glassine packages or tins that were not air tight.

Stores were small wooden buildings located at every crossroads. These buildings certainly did not keep out the weather or pests who enjoyed snack foods and medicines almost as much as people. The traditional answers to these problems for over one hundred years were store jars, tin containers, and glassine packages. No company hoping to penetrate the snack food market could do so successfully without furnishing a protective jar or can.

Store jars probably appeared first in the Northeast in the late 1800s and were nothing more than apothecary jars bearing product names rather than chemical labels. Jars and tins were in wide use across the nation until the late 1950s or early 1960s when some plastic containers appeared. Bulk distribution of cookies was doomed when Nabisco's™ Uneeda Biscuit was first packaged in the In-er-seal™ box, but bulk distribution continued into the 1960s, particularly in rural areas.

The peak years for the use of store jars and tin containers were from 1910 until 1960. Today they have virtually disappeared. The traditional cracker containers were the cracker barrel and box, both wooden in construction. These devices were not conducive to insuring unbroken or fresh products. The conventional story told concerning this problem goes as follows. A store owner was accused of having mice in his cracker barrel to which he replied that he knew it was a lie, as his cat slept there every night.[1] As you can imagine, sanitation was not a major concern.

An English ironmonger named Huntley is credited with manufacturing the first tins in the 1840s. Huntley was the son of the founding Huntley of Huntley and Palmer, a large English bakery.[2] This first tin was improved on by the firm of Vandeveer and Holmes, which developed the glass front tin (adding glass to the lower half of the front below the company logo), allowing consumers to view the product.[3] These were traditionally "brass fronts" (the fronts of the square tin and glass boxes were finished in brass to give a brighter and more attractive appearance) and were used by many major companies. Around World War I, the brass front tin and normal tins were replaced by a cheaper packaging method involving a cardboard box (commonly referred to as a "box front") and a box cover of brass or nickel and glass developed by National Biscuit™.[4] These methods were in turn replaced by the In-er-seal™ box of Nabisco™.[5] At the turn of the century the In-er-seal™ was introduced for small servings.

National Biscuit™ and its precursors led the way in "distribution development" — strategies to increase product sales including improvements in product packaging and transportation systems, to name a few. Most of the northeastern companies were quick to make similar changes. Large companies like the precursors of Continental™, Keebler™, and Sunshine™ were also very quick to follow in adopting new distribution methods. Both the glass front tin and the box front required deposits by the store owner and were recyclable containers.[6]

The origin of the glass jar as a distribution tool is more obscure. Clearly glass jars were in wide use by the late Victorian era. They probably developed as a direct descendant of the apothecary jar used in drug stores. Early in the twentieth century, companies used distinct sizes and shapes of jars with the potbelly being gradually accepted as a standard counter jar. Potbellies were used by Nabisco™, Elephant, Jumbo, and Nut House. These containers continued to evolve until the mid-1930s when the Anchor-Hocking side-loader, and the one and two gallon cylinders became the accepted standards. Few jars made after World War II incorporate different or distinct shapes, but Lance™ and Taylor Biscuit™ are notable exceptions.

The Purpose of This Book

This book is an introduction to the most prominent companies and the containers they used nationally. Northeastern products are well represented and were the first to market nationally. Among the companies using glass jars, only Nut House™, Planter's™, Lance™, and Tom's™ are known to have used jars extensively in the far West and Northwest. The jars shown in this collection are largely Anchor-Hocking standards. The one and two gallon top-loaders and the Anchor-Hocking side-loaders are industry standards and are still available from that company. They became popular in the 1930s and 1940s. Anchor-Hocking was certainly not the only company to produce these jars; it simply is the only one known to still be in production. Laurens Glass in Laurens, South Carolina, was a large producer of these jars, as were hundreds of other small struggling glass companies in the South and Northeast. Tiffin and United States Glass also had versions and were major producers of the potbelly.

A few companies adopted jars that were distinct to their product. Lance™, Taylor Biscuit™, and Planter's™ come to mind immediately; but most simply adopted one or all the standard sizes in use by 1945. It is rare to find a company that used the one or two gallon or the side-loader exclusively, but Quik Snak may be that exception. Ornate jars, apothecary jars, ginger jars, potbellies, and octagon jars are generally earlier in the production cycle with most dating before 1935.

These methods of bulk distribution are largely a thing of the past, but the obscure containers left behind continue to fascinate everyone from housewives with a decorating flair to industrious collectors. Hopefully, this guide will be useful to both.

Introduction Endnotes

[1] William Cahn, *Out of the Cracker Barrel, The Nabisco™ Story, From Animal Crackers to ZuZus,* Simon and Schuster, New York, New York, ISBN: 671-20360-6.
[2] Ibid.
[3] Ibid.
[4] Ibid.
[5] Ibid.
[6] Ibid.

Additional Notes

This started as a regional (Southeastern) effort. But because the marketing needs these jars and tins represented were universal, and the use of these containers was international in development, what started as a Southeastern project quickly grew to include the entire United States. The use of these methods of distribution began in England and the Northeast United States and spread throughout the world. The techniques they represent were replaced as better systems were developed and marketing trends changed. Only in rural areas did they linger on. Perhaps the best explanation as to why these methods remained popular in the rural south, is one that was given to explain regional attitudes in the United States. "The Northeast is provincial and does not know it; the Midwest is provincial and ashamed of the fact; the South, unlike either, is not only provincial but it has fought and will fight for the right to remain so." A less romantic explanation would deal with the poverty inflicted by The War Between the States.

Whatever the reason, the result is that the South has a tendency to cling to things long after their usefulness has been questioned in other places. This writer is proudly and profoundly Southern and hopes that this work will evoke memories for everyone. But it was the backwoods and crossroads of the South of the Great Depression that nurtured and loved these methods of distribution. The lone distributor still using store jars is Tom's™. This company was founded and grew in the heart of the Deep South. These jars and tins are as indicative of the southern backwoods as the Oakeys of John Steinbeck and as southern as William Faulkner. I rather like the idea of one of the Snopes lovingly polishing a nondescript jar in his one-room hardware and general mercantile. Faulkner's book, *The Reivers*, has a wonderful quotation about the peanut parcher man on the waterfront in Memphis that is worth the time spent finding it. This quotation could refer to any one of the wonderful men you will meet here. Since the peanut parcher man is Italian, this quotation immediately evokes visions of Amadeo Obici, standing as a determined, yet frightened, young man on Ellis Island.

It is sad to report that many of these proud companies have been swallowed like Jonah, and they have disappeared into the bowels of the corporate whale. A few of the larger companies like NECCO delight in their history. Correspondingly a few small companies like Tom's™ have emerged from the corporate behemoth with new strength, but most like Gordon's have forgotten not only who they were, but from whence they came. And sadly, some like Dixie have left nothing but the faintest trace of their passage, not unlike a lovingly remembered scent of childhood.

Although not limited to this region, I would offer the following for the consumption of all and as an explanation for my motivation in producing this work:

> "Here's to the south, not just the Old South, but even the New South, both long dead; screen doors on old one-room stores, Moon Pies, R.C. Colas; dirt roads, and tow-headed kids sitting in the beds of rusty pickup trucks, dragging their dirty feet in hot sand or red clay.., and to mules, as well, and red-headed loggers eating dirty bologna and hoop cheese sandwiches by glass-topped gas pumps; a last ode not just for and about plantations and slavery, but mostly a lament about and for the forgotten ones; those who became the middle class; all the rednecks, peckerwoods, and crackers of the piney hills and flat woods. They all got educated and moved to town and alas, they too, are not only gone with the wind; but sadder still, most appear to be ashamed of not only who they are but what they were and from whence they came."

Company Listings

The following companies are covered in this work. If the company does not have a separate section, the parent company in parentheses indicates where the information concerning that company may be found. An asterisk indicates photos or sketches. Bolded companies are featured. Each section on the individual companies includes the following:

I. Brief History (if known)
II. List and Description of known jars and tins
III. Current market price range
IV. Photographs of known jars and tins.
V. Index .

Adams Gum	(American Chicle)	New York, NY
Aldridge Bakery	(Nabisco™)	Chicago, IL
American Biscuit Co.	(Nabisco™)	Chicago, IL
American Chicle Co.		Chicago, IL
Anger Brothers	(Nabisco™)	
Bachman Chocolate Co.	(Hershey)	
Baker's Chocolate *		Dorchester, MA
Beeman's Chewing Gum	(American Chicle)	OH
Beich's Candy *		Chicago, IL
Belle-Meade Biscuit	(Keebler™)	Nashville, TN
Bent and Co. Biscuits	(Nabisco™)	Milton, MA
Big Block	(Hershey)	
Binckerhoff and Co.	(Nabisco™)	
Blue Bell Potato Chips	(Sunshine™)	Portland, OR
Bob's *		Albany, GA
Bowman Biscuit	(Keebler™)	Denver, CO
Bremner Bakery	(Nabisco™)	Chicago, IL
Brennon Foods		Atlanta, GA
Bunte™ Candy *		Chicago, IL
Burlington Bread Co.	(Nabisco™)	Burlington, VT
Byrd Cookies *		Savannah, GA
Cadbury Candies	(Hershey)	Britain
Camp's Foods *		
Carpenter & Underwood	(Nabisco™)	Milwaukee, WI
Charles Chips *		PA, KY
Charleston Biscuit		Charleston, S.C.
Chattanooga Bakery *		Chattanooga, TN
Chase Candy Company	(NECCO)	Boston, MA
Christie, Brown, & Co.	(Nabisco™)	Toronto, Canada.
Cleveland Bakery	(Nabisco™)	Cleveland, OH
Colgan Chewing Gum	(American Chicle)	Louisville, KY
Colonial Biscuit *	(Nabisco™)	Pittsburgh, PA
Continental Baking Co.		Chicago, IL
Crawford and Zeller	(Nabisco™)	Mansfield, OH
Cream of Wheat	(Nabisco™)	MN
Curtiss Candies *	(Nabisco™) (Nestle)	Chicago, IL
Dad's Cookies *		
Daggett Chocolate	(Necco)	Cambridge, MA
Dale-Care Bakery	(Nabisco™)	

Daniel Canty Bakers	(Nabisco™)	
Decatur Biscuit Co.	(Nabisco™)	IL
Dietrich Candy Inc.	(Hershey)	
Dickey's Foods	(Sunshine™)	New Orleans, LA
Dixie Biscuit *		Atlanta, GA
Dove Candies	(M&M * Mars)	Chicago, IL
Dozier Baking Co.	(Nabisco™)	St. Louis, MO
Drenk's Foods		Milwaukee, WI
Duke Sandwich		Greenville, S.C.
Elephant Peanuts		
Elliott Bakery	(Nabisco™)	
Ethel M. Chocolates Inc.	(M&M * Mars)	Las Vegas, NE
F. Hoffman and Co.	(Leaf)	Chicago, IL
F.A. Martoccio Co.	(Leaf)	
F.H. Bennett Biscuit Co.	(Nabisco™)	New York, N.Y.
Fargo Biscuit Company	(Keebler™)	Fargo, S.D.
Fiesta Foods	(Sunshine™)	Phoenix, AZ
Felber Biscuit	(Keebler™)	Columbus, OH
Fisher Nuts *™		Cincinnati, OH
Fobe & Hayward Candy	(Necco)	Boston, MA
Frito-Lay Chips *™		Plano, TX
Golden, Co.	(Leaf)	
Golden Flake Foods *™		Lakeview, TX
Goodest Foods		Abbeville, S.C.
Gordon's Chips *™		Louisville, KY
H.B. Reese Candy Co.	(Hershey)	Hershey, PA
Hamilton Co.	(Nabisco™)	N.J.
Heath Brothers	(Leaf)	Robinson, IL
Hekman Biscuit	(Keebler™)	Grand Rapids, IA
Hershey Chocolate		Hershey, PA
Hetfield and Ducker	(Nabisco™)	
Holland Rusk Co.	(Nabisco™)	Holland, MI
Hollywood Brands	(Leaf)	
Holmes and Coutts	(Nabisco™)	
Huntley and Palmer	(Nabisco™)	Britian
Illinois Baking Co.	(Keebler™)	IL
Iten Biscuit Co.	(Nabisco™)	Omaha, NB
Iten-Barmettler Biscuit	(Keebler™)	
J.N. Collins Co.	(Hershey)	
Jake's Peanut *	(Brennon Foods)	Atlanta, GA
Jacob and Co.	(Nabisco™)	Ireland
James O. Welch Candies	(Nabisco™)	
J.D. Gilmore and Co.	(Nabisco™)	
J.D. Mason and Co.	(Nabisco™)	Baltimore, MD
John Pearson Baker	(Nabisco™)	Boston, MA
Jolly Rancher	(Leaf)	
Johnston Bakery		Milwaukee, WI
Jumbo (Dixie Brand) Peanuts		Boston, MA
Kansas City Baking Co.	(Nabisco™)	Kansas City, MO
Keebler™ - Weyl Biscuit	(Keebler™)	Philadelphia, PA
Keebler™ Co.		Elmhurst, IL
Kennedy Biscuit Works	(Nabisco™)	Boston, MA
Kis-me Gum	(American Chicle)	
Klein's Foods	(Sunshine™)	Chicago, IL
Koller & Barret	(Hershey)	Reading, PA

Krun-chee Foods*	(Sunshine™)	Detroit, MI
Lakeside Biscuit Co.	(Keebler™)	Toledo, OH
Lance™		Charlotte, N.C.
Langeles Bakery	(Nabisco™)	New Orleans, LA
Larrabee Co.	(Nabisco™)	
Leaf Candies		
Lillibridge-Bremer Baking	(Nabisco™)	Minneapolis, MN
Lifesavers Candy	(Nabisco™)	Cleveland, OH
Lion Peanut		Chicago, IL.
Loose-Wiles Biscuit*	(Sunshine™)	Kansas City
Lovell and Covel Candy	(Necco)	
M&M * Mars		N.J.
Manchester Biscuit	(Keebler™)	Fargo, S.D.
Mann Potato Chip	(Sunshine™)	Washington, DC
Marvin Baking Co.	(Nabisco™)	Pittsburgh, PA
Mars	(M&M * Mars)	Chicago, IL
McClurg & Co. Crackers		Allegheny, PA
Mclaren Cones	(Nabisco™)	Dayton, OH
Maryland Biscuit Co.	(Murray)	Baltimore, MD
Meadors' Manufacturing Co. *		Greenville, S.C.
Merchants Biscuit Co.		Omaha, NB
Miller Bakery	(Nabisco™)	
Moore's Chips *		Bristol, VA
Monarch*		Chicago/New York
Mitchum and Tucker *		Charlotte, N.C.
Nabisco™ *		Chicago, IL
National Cracker Co.	(Nabisco™)	Cedar Rapids, IA
National Licorice Co.	(Hershey)	Brooklyn, N.Y.
National Biscuit Company	(Nabisco™)	Chicago, IL
Nestle, USA		CA
New England Confectionery Co. *		Cambridge, MA
New Haven Baking Co.	(Nabisco™)	New Haven, CT
New York Biscuit Co.	(Nabisco™)	New York, N.Y.
Nut House		Cambridge, MA
Old Vienna Products	(Sunshine™)	St. Louis, MO
Old World Baking Co.	(Keebler™)	Michigan City, MI
Ontario Biscuit Co.	(Keebler™)	Buffalo, N.Y.
OK Brands	(Wright & Moody)	Boston, MA
Overland Candy Co.	(Leaf)	
Oxford Biscuit Fabrik	(Nabisco™)	Hjorring, Denmark
Page and Shaw	(Necco)	Boston, MA
Parks and Savage	(Nabisco™)	Hartford, CT
Polly Parrot Potato Chips	(Hiland)	Sioux Falls, S.D.
Peter Paul*	(Cadbury/ Hershey)	CT
Petherbridge & Scudder Bros.	(Hershey)	New York, N.Y.
Planter's™*		Suffolk, VA
Poinsettia Chips	(Meadors' ?)	Greenville, S.C.
Purity Biscuit Co.	(Keebler™)	Salt Lake City, UT
Quality Biscuit Co.	(Keebler™)	Milwaukee, WI
Quality Baking	(Virginia Baking)	Richmond , VA
Quaker City Confectionery*	(Leaf)	
Quik Sank*		Western N.C.
Ramon's Medicine*		Le Roy, N.Y.
Rawl's Foods*		Winston-Salem, N.C.
Richmond Baking Co.*		Richmond, VA
Rowntree Mcintosh	(Hershey)	Britain
Sawyer Biscuit Co.	(Keebler™)	Melrose Park
Sommer-Richards on Baking	(Nabisco™)	St. Louis, MO
Southern Biscuit Company *		Richmond, VA
Supreme Bakery	(Keebler™)	
Schuler's Foods	(Sunshine™)	Rochester, N.Y.
Sioux Falls Biscuit Co.	(Keebler™)	Sioux Falls, S.D.
Standard Biscuit Co. *		Des Moines, IA
Strietmann's Biscuit	(Keebler™)	Cincinnati, OH
Sunshine™ Biscuits *		Kansas City/N.J.
Squirrel Nuts *		Cambridge, MA
Stewart's Sandwiches *		Norfolk, VA
Swinson's Food Products *		Charlotte, N.C.
Switzer	(Leaf)	
Taggart Baking Company	(Continental)	Indianapolis, IN
Taylor Biscuit™ *		Raleigh, N.C.
Tom's™ Foods *		Columbus, GA
Tennessee Biscuit Co.	(Keebler™)	Nashville, TN
Terry's Chips *		Bristol, TN
Treadwell and Harris	(Nabisco™)	New York, N.Y.
Uneeda Biscuit Co.	(Nabisco™)	Chicago, IL
Union Biscuit Co.	(Keebler™)	St. Louis, MO
United Bakeries Inc.	(Continental)	Chicago, IL
United Biscuit Co.	(Keebler™)	Melrose Park, IL
United States Baking Co.	(Nabisco™)	Philadelphia, PA
Vandeveer and Holmes	(Nabisco™)	
Virginia Baking Co. *		Richmond, VA
Virginia Dare Sandwiches *		Eastern N.C.
W. H. Johnson Candy Co.	(Hershey)	
Walker's Crisps	(Nabisco™)	Britain
Walla Walla Gum		Knoxville, TN
Ward Baking Company	(Continental)	New York, N.Y.
Ward Johnston Candy	(Nestle)	Chicago, IL
Wickham Potato Chip Co.	(Sunshine™)	Selbyville, DE
Williamson Candy Co.	(Nestle)	Chicago, IL
Wilson Biscuit Co.	(Nabisco™)	Philadelphia, PA
Winters and Co.	(Hershey)	Philadelphia, PA
Wise Chips	(Borden) *	Atlanta, GA
W.P. Ihrie and Sons	(Sunshine™)	Baltimore, MD
Wright & Moody Candy	(Necco)	Boston, MA
Wrigley Co.		Chicago, IL
Y & S Candies	(Hershey)	Brooklyn, N.Y.
York Cone Co.	(Hershey)	
York Pretzel	(Nabisco™)	York, PA
Yucatan Gum	(American Chicle)	Cleveland, OH

Companies and Their Counter Jars

American Chicle Co.
1899

The American Chicle Company was formed in 1899, when William White of Yucatan Gum, Thomas Adams, Jr. of Adams Gum, Dr. Edward Beeman of Beeman's Gum, Jonathan Primley of Kis-Me Gum, and gum maker S.T. Britten joined forces to form a chewing gum giant. William White became the company president, and Thomas Adams, Jr. was chairman of the board of directors. Today, the company is a division of Warner-Lambert.

Adams Gum™
New York City
circa 1870s

The fathers of the modern American chewing gum business were Thomas Adams Sr. and Antonio Lopez de Santa Anna of Alamo fame. While in exile from Mexico, Santa Anna lived in New York and boarded with the Adams family on Staten Island. Santa Anna had an idea that he thought the inventive Adams could turn into a fortune.

Chicle was the gummy substance that people in Mexico extracted from the Sapota tree. Santa Anna thought it could be used to make the rubber for carriage tires. He had his friends in Mexico send Adams a ton of chicle to develop the idea. Adams and his son, Thomas, experimented to no avail. Discouraged, Adams decided to consign the ton of chicle to storage and determined to be rid of it by dumping the mess into the East River. Adams was neither the first nor the last to consider consigning a problem to that river. Fortunately fate provided other options.

One day, shortly after reaching his decision, Adams went to a drugstore and overheard a young patron buy a penny's worth of White Mountain Gum made from paraffin. To Adams, who knew about chewing chicle, this seemed a more profitable method of disposal than dumping the mess in the river. Adams and his son, Thomas Jr., then decided to package, label, and name the gum. Thomas Jr. could peddle it on his route as a salesman of wholesale tailors supplies. The creation was named Adams, New York No. 1. It was unflavored and wrapped in tissue paper. On the cover of the box was a picture of the City Hall of New York.

Thomas Jr. started west with 25 boxes of gum and was unable to sell any on the first trip. However, the Adams family still had a ton of chicle to sell, store, or pitch. On his next trip Adams resolved to give the gum to the druggists he called on and leave the information on how to reorder. Before he returned to New York his father had reorders for about three hundred boxes. The business was moved to New Jersey and about twenty-five or thirty young women were hired to wrap gum. Other brands followed including Adams No. 2, which was a larger package and Adams Sapota.

Colgan Chewing Gum
Louisville, Ky.
1879

John Colgan was a druggist in Louisville whose store was located at the corner of Tenth and Walnut streets. Aware of Thomas Adams' success and the popularity of balsam gum flavored with powdered sugar, Colgan ordered 100 pounds of chicle from Central America. What he got was 1,500 pounds and an ultimatum to accept the entire shipment. Colgan then developed Colgan's Taffy Tolu Chewing Gum — an overnight success. Colgan sold the drug store and turned his attention to the development of chewing gum. One cannot help wondering what would have happened if he had been forced to dump his chicle in the Ohio River.

Beeman's Chewing Gum™
Ohio

Dr. Edward E. Beeman was the manufacturer of Beeman's Pepsin Powder, a patent medicine that was sold as an aid to digestion. His bookkeeper, Nellie Horton, suggested that he put pepsin powder into gum because, "People buy pepsin to aid digestion and gum for no reason at all." Dr. Beeman then began to blend his pepsin powder with chicle and marketed the gum under his logo — a pig, using his motto "With pepsin, you can eat like a pig." Beeman's product did well but a financier reorganized the Beeman company and replaced the pig on the wrapper with Dr. Beeman's face.

Yucatan Gum
Cleveland, Ohio 1880

William J. White, a popcorn salesman from Cleveland, had come into possession of a barrel of chicle that a neighborhood grocer had received instead of the barrel of nuts he ordered. White began to experiment at home with the chicle. Chicle, he found, would not hold flavor but sugar would. Soon he discovered that by combining the flavors with corn syrup, any flavor could be obtained. White chose peppermint and called the new product Yucatan Gum. Mr. White then went to Washington to promote his product by giving every member of Congress a box of his gum. White fell in love with politics and successfully ran for Congress. Ever the promoter, he then built a steam yacht and sailed to England. Receiving an audience with King Edward VII, he presented His Majesty with a box of Yucatan and gave the monarch a sales pitch, all of which was cabled back to the American news. Before he finished, White was known as the P.T. Barnum of chewing gum.

Kis-me Gum

Kis-me Gum was developed by Jonathan P. Primley as a method to overcome the idea that no "nice girl" would ever chew. Primley developed the first fruit-flavored gum and named it Kis-me in a stroke of marketing genius. He advertised under the premise that if a girl asked for a stick of his gum, the boy could always steal a kiss, having misunderstood the request.

Other gums that joined American Chicle

In the year of the formation of the American Chicle Company Franklin V. Canning, the manager of a New York drug store, teamed up with a dentist to develop a gum that would promote good dental health. After much effort, he developed a pink gum that was a combination of ingredients he and the dentist found to be the most healthy. The name chosen combined the words dental hygiene and became Dentyne.

In 1916, American Chicle acquired the Dentyne Company. In 1914, American Chicle bought a candy-coated gum that was conceived of by a candy salesman and based on candy-coated almonds. The product name was Chiclet and had been developed around the turn of the century.

Adams Clove Gum™ was developed at the time of prohibition and was able to help the many avoid the few by letting "Adams Clove take your breath away." (All trademarks and slogans are the sole property of the American Chicle Division of the Warner-Lambert Company.)

The information in this article was graciously furnished by Warner-Lambert and can be found in "The Story of Chewing Gum, Warner-Lambert, Morris Plains, New Jersey."

Chewing Gum Jars

Early chewing gum jars are patterned after the apothecary jars normally associated with turn of the century drug stores. These jars normally feature a ground lid that seals tightly. Most of the marked jars have the product name etched or embossed in the glass. Kiss-me, Beeman's, Colgan, and Adams all used jars of this type. The glass was very thin and any damage or replacement lid absolutely destroys the value. These jars are frequently seen offered for sale in the $75-$150 range but top end prices usually include an early label and perfect condition that adds a premium to the value.

Walla-Walla Gum from Knoxville,Tennessee is a premium jar because of the Indian portrayed in the embossed glass. This jar with excellent definition in the embossing and excellent condition can bring several hundred dollars. However, any price over $500.00 should be viewed with a jaundiced eye and under no circumstances should any damaged jar bring more than a very small fraction of top value.

A method of marking apothecary jars using modern transfer letters has been adopted and marketed as a type of early drug store jar. A fantasy Planter's™ jar based on the Anchor-Hocking standard one-gallon and an apothecary marked Wrigley's have both been encountered. Since transfer lettering of this type was not available until the 1980s, they are easily identified. Unlike fired on letters, these letters will usually display a white

backing on the inside of the jar and are always raised much too high for a fired-on feel or appearance.

Armour's Star Meat™ Bouillon Cubes

Armour Meats produced a single side-loading jar for the distribution of bouillon cubes. This jar is not common in the South and when seen is usually priced between $40-$60. The lid was a standard tin lid and is often missing. The lettering is white.

Armour Side Loader — Flip Lid.

Armour Meats Side Loader, circa 1950.

Aunt Jane's Candy Treats

Baker's with the portrait in white on a one gallon Anchor-Hocking standard jar — $40-$75.

Baker's Chocolate One Gallon Circular Standard.

Aunt Jane's Candy Treats — this jar was observed with a lid that fit poorly; it is unknown if the lid shown is the correct one or if the jar was uncovered, which seems unlikely.

Baker's Chocolate One Gallon, Dorchester Massachusetts, circa 1950.

Baker's Chocolate One Gallon, view of trademark, circa 1950.

Baker's Chocolate™ 1764-

Walter Baker's mill was founded in 1764. From this humble beginning Baker's products expanded, but it was his chocolate and cocoa products that made the company famous. His logo was modeled on Jean-Etienne Liotard's portrait of Anna Baltaug, a Viennese waitress who married a prince. The aristocrat then commissioned Liotard for the portrait that Baker adopted as his emblem. General Foods purchased the company in 1927 and primary production of the product is still in Dorchester, Massachusetts.

Beich's Candy ™
St. Louis, Missouri

The Kathryn Beich Fund-Raising Company and Beich Company were acquired by Nestle in 1984. Laffy-Taffy™, one of Beich's most celebrated products, carried the Beich name until 1994 when it was deleted by the company currently controlling its manufacture. Generations of school children alternately cherish and detest the shared memory of selling Beich peppermint and peanut butter pillows door-to-door. Many of the tins survive today holding two marbles, a piece of crayon, a broken pen, a bent photograph, and all the other momentos of forgotten childhood.

Beich Swirl Lid, circa 1910.

Beich Logo as embossed on both Beich Jars.

Beich Paneled Candy.

Beich Paneled with Swirl Lid, circa 1910.

Beich paneled barrel jar, embossed Beich's with correct lid — $85-$150.

Bob's™
Albany, Georgia

In 1918, the Gatsby generation returned from "the war to end all wars, "and among them was a young lieutenant named Bob McCormack. Lt. McCormack, like so many young men of his generation, had a dream and his was to manufacture candy. Mr. McCormack had grown up in the South in the cities of Nashville and Birmingham, but had a deep desire to seek his destiny in a smaller community. Like the hero in *The Razor's Edge*, Mr. McCormack began to travel, seeking a community in which to build that dream. On a train to Jackson, Mississippi, a stranger suggested Albany, Georgia as "an up-and-coming little town," and Bob McCormack agreed. It was here that he opened the "Famous Candy Company™," in April of 1919.

The name was soon changed to "Bob's™." The company began with five employees including Mr. McCormack, who served as salesman, bookkeeper, and plant manager. In spite of the economic crash of the price of cotton following World War I, sound management and hard work made the small company a success. Steady production of quality products led to growth of the product line. Fudge, stick candy, coconut bars, and peanut products were all included as the new company grew. However pecan candy was the specialty of the company in its early years. Always an innovator, Bob's was the first candy manufacturer in the United States to use cellophane, imported at this early date from the Alsace region of France.

The crash of 1929 affected Bob's in much the same way as it did the entire South where depression had been the rule since the cotton crash in 1919. The 1930s brought changes in methods of distribution and Bob's featured display jars with tin lids. The products packaged this way included coconut ices, Bob's clear stick candy in a variety of flavors, Bob's sensation balls, Bob's peanut squares, Bob's sour balls, and Bob's mint breathers. Distribution, under sound management, had continued to grow as the South urbanized and recovered.

The year 1940 brought a catastrophe to the Albany community that a lesser company or man would not have survived. A tornado demolished the company and over seven hundred truckloads of debris were removed from the former factory site. Bob McCormack began again and, later that year, Bob's was back in operation and growing. World War II brought sugar rationing and Bob's expanded into the area of cracker sandwiches and peanut products to bring in additional sales. The first machine to make cracker sandwiches automatically was developed and patented at Bob's.

Thousands of pounds of special hard candies were manufactured for the war effort, but price ceilings forced the company out of the pecan candy market. After the war Bob's resumed its full range of products. In 1947 Bob's offered their dealers the standard side-loading jar with Bob's logo for 95 cents each. The other jars used by Bob's were the less costly tin screw-top jars with paper labels, commonly referred to as "biscuit jars."

The fifties saw a development that changed the direction of the company. A machine to make stick candy automatically was invented and patented at Bob's. The "Keller machine" was invented by Mrs. McCormack's brother, Father Gregory Keller, a Catholic priest for whom inventing was a hobby. A machine to make candy canes quickly followed and Bob's began to specialize in the manufacture of stick candy. Packaging was designed to accommodate the shipping of the delicate product. Bob's

gradually became the acknowledged leader in the field of stick candy production and the largest producer of stick candy and candy canes in the world — a position it retains today.

In 1986, Bob's produced a one-gallon Anchor-Hocking standard jar with the Bob's logo on one side and the carriage logo on the opposite; probably as an appeal to a growing nostalgia market. Bob's is still independent and under the management and control of the McCormack family. In a world of corporate giants we hope it can remain that way.

All trademarks and slogans and the sole property of Bob's. Our special thanks to Bee McCormack, who provided the information in this history and did detailed research on Bob's use of jars that has made this company's history one of the most complete in this series.

Standard, Anchor-Hocking, one gallon, Bob's, Albany, Ga. Peanut Butter Sandwiches, Salted Peanuts — $35-$50.

Standard side-loader, Bob's, Albany Ga. Peanut Butter Sandwiches, Salted Peanuts — $35-$50. Sold in 1947 to jobbers (see following pages).

Albany, Ga.

Peanut Butter Sandwiches

Salted Peanuts

Bob's 1947 Jobbers Jar a standard side-loader with flip lid. This logo is also seen on a standard one gallon jar.

Bob's Side Loader, 1947.

One gallon standard, Bob's, Makers of Pure Candy, Albany Ga., 1986 Collector's Series — $25-$35.

Bob's Logo as seen on the One Gallon Circular

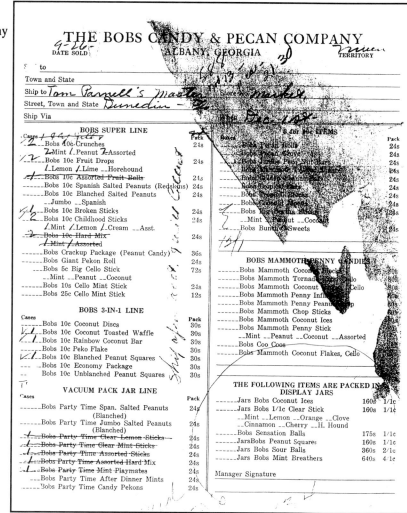

List of Bob's products, circa 1934.

Bob's One Gallon, 1986.

View of both Bob's older Side Loader and more recent One Gallon.

View of Bob's products, circa late 1940s.

Packed assorted (as illustrated) or straight flavors—
Cherry, Orange, Lemon, Lime, Cinnamon

Guaranteed 300 count.....Packed 4 jars to case.....Priced at $ 1.80 per jar
Minimum shipment for full freight allowance, 24 jars.

- -

Dear Bob: Please ship me _____ cases BOBS SENSATION BALLS packed as follows:

____Lemon ____Lime ____Cherry ____Orange ____Cinnamon ____Assorted

Signed_____ Address_____

Bob's 1949 jar offer.

OF
Fall 47'

COURSE

IT'S

Bobs

HERE'S A REAL HOLIDAY TREAT

(BOBS JAR-O-SWEETS IS A BIG (8 IN.), BEAUTIFUL UTILITY DECANTER PACKED FULL (ABOUT
2 LB.) OF BOBS FINE CRUNCHY SATIN FINISH HARD CANDY. A PERSONAL ITEM, A HOUSEHOLD
ITEM, A GIFT ITEM!) THE CLEAR YELLOW, RED, GREEN, ROSE, AND WHITE OF THE SATIN FINISH
CANDY AND THE SPARKLING BEAUTY OF THE CONTAINER MAKE THIS A TRULY EYE-CATCHING,
SALES-CATCHING PACKAGE! BOBS JAR-O-SWEETS IS PACKED 4 JARS TO THE CASE AND IS PRICED
AT $3.52 PER CASE DELIVERED. ORDER NOW FOR NOVEMBER AND EARLY DECEMBER SHIPMENT.

Dear Bob:

Please ship me _____ cases of BOBS JAR-O-SWEETS at $3.52 per case, delivered.

Signed_____ Address_____

IT'S Bobs FOR QUALITY
ALBANY, GA.

Bob's 1947 jar offer.

Bobs

PENNY JAR CANDIES

GUARANTEED COUNT   225 OR OVER

Packed 4 jars to case
straight or assorted

Price per jar $1.35 full freight allowed
on shipments of 200 lb. or more. (200# = 8 cs.)

SUGGESTION

Order these four jar items packed assorted
to one case. Instruct your salesmen to
carry a full case into customer's store.
These four assorted jars make a beautiful
and sales-attracting display in any store.

- -

Dear Bob: Please ship me;

____Cs. Mint Lumps   ____Cs. Asst. Lumps   ____Cs. Mint Sticks

____Cs. Lemon Sticks   ____Asst. Cases

Signed_____ Address_____

Mail this order to BOBS CANDY & PEANUT CO., INC., ALBANY, GA.

Bob's 1949 jar offer.

Bobs
MINT
LUMPS

A REAL VALUE
IN A PENNY ITEM!

Bob's 1949 jar offer.

- SATIN FINISHED
- PLENTY OF FLAVOR
- GOOD REPEATER

PACKED 250 PIECES TO
GALLON GLASS JAR AT

$1.35 PER JAR DELIVERED
4 JARS TO SHIPPING CASE
8 CASES MINIMUM SHIPMENT
WITH FULL FREIGHT ALLOWED

PLACE YOUR ORDER TODAY

- -

Dear Bob: Please ship immediately

____Jars BOBS MINT LUMPS, 250 count, 4 jars to case, priced at $1.35 per jar delivered.

Signed_____ Firm_____ Address_____

MR. JOBBER

Get your share of Peanut Butter Sandwiches and Salted Peanut Business.

Place a Jar with your Customer, then keep it filled with BOBS and watch your Sales increase.

Jars as shown can be supplied in any quantity shipped with your Sandwich or Peanut order, costing 95c each.

BOBS: Please ship _____Jars with my next order

Signed_____

Address_____

Bob's 1947 jar offer.

Bob's 1951 jar offer.

I CASE FREE WITH 20 CASES
ON
Bobs
SPRING
PROFIT-BOOSTER DEAL

Delicious assorted fruit
balls—finest flavors,
clear colors.

Crunchy peanut brittle
squares dipped in
sugar icing.

Moist mello coconut
center dipped in

Here's how you can boost your profits for the Spring months — Beginning March 15, and ending May 1, Bobs is offering a real cost reduction on 3 fast moving jar items—

Bobs Asst. Sensation Balls ___4 jars to cs.
　　　　　　　　—Appr. 300 ct. _____ 1.80 per jar
Bobs Nutty Ices _____4 jars to cs.
　　　　　　　　—Appr. 300 ct. _____ 1.80 per jar
Bobs Coconut Ices _____4 jars to cs.
　　　　　　　　—Appr. 250 ct. _____1.60 per jar
Above prices are delivered

Here's the Deal!

YOU BUY 20 cases of any one or combination of the above jar items at the price listed.

BOBS WILL SEND YOU FREE 1 case of Coconut Ices.

BOBS CAN ACCEPT ONLY ONE ORDER ON THIS SPRING-PROFIT-BOOSTER DEAL. HOWEVER;

YOU MAY INCLUDE AS MANY DEALS AS YOU WISH ON YOUR ONE ORDER AS LONG AS ALL SHIPMENTS ARE COMPLETED BY MAY 1, 1952.

ALSO—A deal may be divided into 2 shipments of 10 cases each. In this case free goods will go with the last shipment on each deal.

Increase your Spring Profits with Bobs Spring-Profit-Booster Deal. Use the handy Postcard order enclosed.

BOBS CANDY & PEANUT CO.

16

Brach's Candy Company

Brach's box front, circa 1930-1960, $15-$25.

Brach's Pure Candy

Brach's chose to use an impressed frame
that could not be altered. They also changed
the standard arrangement or layout by
placing the script at the bottom of the frame.
The letters are silver on a red background in
a silver frame.

Brach's Box Front, circa 1930-1960.

Bray Candy and Peanut Company

One gallon standard, Anchor-Hocking, embossed in bottom as shown $15-$25.

Bottom Bray's Candy and Peanut One Gallon Circular

Bray's Jar Bottom, paper or decal label jar.

Bunte™ *Candy*
Chicago
1876

Bunte™ Candy Apothecary — a paneled jar with embossed script Bunte™, probably manufactured by the same glass company as the Beich paneled jar — $125-$200.

Bunte™ Candy Apothecary — the circular jar with embossed script Bunte™, ground lid but much less ornate than the above — $100-$175.

Bunte Logo as embossed on Bunte Jar.

Bunte Circular Apothecary, circa 1910-1930.

Bunte Circular Apothecary.

Bunte Paneled
Apothecary, circa
1890-1930.

Bunte Paneled Apothecary.

Bunte™ Upright tin — manufactured in a variety of colors and logos for different candy lines. Illustrates the factory and had a screw-on tin lid — $20-$35.

Bunte Small Embossed Candy, circa 1895-1925.

Bunte Tin (top view), circa 1895.

Bunte Tin (view of front with paper label), circa 1910-1935.

Bunte Tin (side view), circa 1910-1935.

Bunte Tin (front view), circa 1895.

Bunte Tin (rear view), circa 1895.

Current Bunte Tin, circa 1990.

Bunte Small Candy Jar.

Byrd's Two Gallon, Savannah, Georgia, circa 1955.

Camp's Foods

Camp's Foods - Red Letter logo, Standard Anchor Hocking two gallon marked Camp's Foods — $35-$60.

Byrd Cookies
Savannah, Georgia

Byrd Cookies Savannah, Georgia — Red Letter Logo, standard Anchor Hocking two gallon marked Byrd's Famous Cookies — $35-$60.

Byrd's tins — $5-$10.

Byrd's Famous Cookies Logo as found on Two Gallon Circular.

Camp' Logo as found on the Camp's Two Gallon Circular.

Camp's Two Gallon, circa 1955.

Charles Chips
Pennsylvania

Charles Chips is known primarily for its tins. Many variations of the Charles Chips tin exist, including one with a brief history of the company. Most of the tins found in the South indicate manufacture and packing in Kentucky.

Charles Tins, 1950-1990.

Charles Nuts — $15; Charles Chips — $5-$10; Charles Cookies — $5-$10.

Claussen's Pickles™

Claussen's is currently using an Anchor-Hocking standard jar for deli sales. The two-gallon jar costs about $50 in antique shops and the one gallon about half that amount. You can probably order these through your local supermarket at a considerable discount.

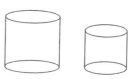

Claussen Logo similar to the logo found on both current jars.

Claussen Two Gallon Standard Jar.

Chattanooga Bakery
Chattanooga, Tennessee
1903-

In 1919, the story goes, a tired traveling salesman walked into the Chattanooga Bakery in Chattanooga, Tennessee. Times were tough in the Deep South following World War I, and there was a drop in cotton prices that marked the beginning of a trend of economic collapse that would continue until World War II. The salesman had no idea of the future as he cast his eyes about the offerings for sale in the bakery and was unable to find anything to suit his taste. When the clerk inquired if he could help, the man replied that what he had in mind was a couple of soft cookies with a little marshmallow between, covered in chocolate. Softly he sighed, and said the immortal words, "I expect a man would have to go to the moon to get a pie like that." The clerk and bakery thought this sounded like a wonderful idea and felt the moon was much too far to go for a treat they could make and market in Tennessee.

From these humble origins rose the harvest moon and great-granddaddy of all Southern snack foods, The MOON PIE™. Sam Campbell IV, like any good Southerner, knows and understands that here in a world of cavaliers and maidens, a good legend is always better than musty old history. What might have happened is that a dusty salesman tired of trying to compete in a world of similar products came into the home office and said, "What would sell in my region is a product that looks bigger and costs the same. Now, if we could take a couple of big graham cracker cookies and put marshmallow in-between and cover it with chocolate, then make it as big as the moon, we could take

the market from these chumps in the cookie business." Whatever happened, a legend was born and just in time for the Great Depression. MOON PIE™ and R.C. Cola™ found the ultimate solution for any marketing problem ... give a little more for the same price. From that idea grew the plowboy's lunch — an R.C. Cola™ and a MOON PIE™, all that for just a dime.

The story of Chattanooga Bakery begins around 1903 when Mountain City Flour Mill decided to go lateral to dispose of excess flour. During the early years, the bakery produced over one hundred and fifty varieties of cookies, crackers, fig bars, iced and animal cookies. Operating until 1939 under the Lookout Cross logo, Chattanooga Bakery probably has many non-standard store jars. It was an early company and a large one. The current logo became a part of Chattanooga Bakery in 1939. The primary market in the early years was up the mountain chain to West Virginia and down to Atlanta. Today the market is worldwide.

Chattanooga Bakery is still a family business, run by the dynamic Campbell family with Sam the Fourth at the helm. It is still run the family way. A fine example is the one paymistress who served under four generations of the Campbell family.

In a world that is steadily encroaching on the South, it is good to know that some things stay the same. So, savor a bit of your past and help save the good things from a dying South at the same time. Treat yourself ... go buy a Moonpie™ and an R.C., sit on the curb or steps of a store, and remember.

Little is known about the store jars of Chattanooga Bakery, the tin illustrates the Lookout Cross logo from the twenties. Chattanooga Bakery is one of the older companies in the Deep South. Its identification with a specific product and the age of the company seem to assure the existence of a great variety of packaging, but locating examples of jars and tins remains an elusive quest.

"Moon Pie™" is a registered trademark of Chattanooga Bakery, where applicable trademarks and slogans are licensed, protected, and the sole property of the companies. Special thanks to Mr. Sam Campbell IV and the Chattanooga Library. These sources furnished the majority of the information found in this article. The Moonpie Culture Club no longer exists at the address furnished in *The Moonpie Book*, but the best among the Moonpie culture need no handbook, especially those who love it so deeply.

The pictured tin was located in an East Tennessee barn. Large Lookout Cross logo tins, $30-$45.

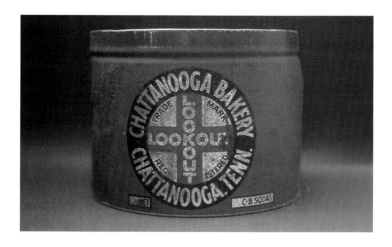

Chattanooga Bakery Tin with the Lookout Cross logo, circa 1925.

Chattanoga Bakery's Lookout Cross Logo.

Continental Baking Company
Chicago, Illinois
1924

The Continental Baking Company was formed in 1924 by William B. Ward. Mr. Ward's grandfather and father were both bakers and his grandfather founded Ward Baking Company in 1849. By 1912, they were managing a thirty million dollar combination of Eastern and Midwestern bakeries. In 1921 William Ward left Ward Bakeries to promote United Bakeries Inc. which became the nucleus of Continental. Within a matter of years, United Bakeries had acquired nine large baking companies including Ward Baking. By 1927 one hundred and four companies were controlled by Continental Baking representing both the United States and Canada.

Continental introduced a number of pioneer concepts in the bread industry, many of which remain as centerpieces of its product line. Most notably, it was the first company to market sliced bread. It was also a driving force behind government efforts to market enriched bread. The latter idea led to the virtual elimination of beriberi and pellagra in this nation.

An early acquisition of Continental was Taggart Baking Company of Indianapolis (1925). Taggart produced colorfully wrapped Wonder Bread™ that became the national bread line of Continental. In 1930 sliced bread was introduced nationally, and Continental also began to market the Twinkie Snack Cake and Hostess Donut lines. Continental is unaware of who actually developed these lines. However, D.R. Rice originated the first chocolate cupcake without filling for Taggart in 1919. Hostess™ was registered as a trademark by William Ward in 1925. In 1930, Jimmy Dewar, a Chicago-area regional manager, saw a need for a new, low-priced product that could be successfully marketed in the Depression. He was also aware that the Conti-

nental shortcake pans were idle during most of the year. His idea was to inject the same cakes with a filling and market them year-round. From a billboard he had seen in St. Louis, he evolved the Twinkie™ name.

Continental was involved in a government project in the thirties and forties that became known as the Quiet Miracle. Enrichment of bread was touted as the great secret weapon in a war on disease, and by the end of World War II virtually all bread in the United States was enriched.

Continental moved heavily into the snack food market following World War II. Sno Balls™ were introduced in 1947. Each Sno Ball™ consists of a chocolate cupcake with white creme filling covered with a marshmallow and coconut mixture. The color of Sno Balls™ differs from season to season. Each of Continental's forty-seven bakeries vary the color from white to pink. Throughout the year other colors are used: green for St. Patrick's day, orange for Halloween and yellow for Easter. Hostess Suzy Q's™ were created by Paul Vance and "Doc" Rice in 1961 and first distributed nationally in 1962.

The Suzy Q™ is an oblong sandwich of banana-flavored yellow cake or devil's food cake with a white creme filling. It was named after the daughter of Continental's vice-president, Cliff Isaacson. Fruit pies for Continental were created by Cliff Isaacson and "Doc" Rice in 1962 and were originally offered in cherry, apple, pineapple and lemon. Peach, blueberry, berry, strawberry, and French apple were added later. Ding Dongs™ were introduced in the mid-sixties and named by the company's marketing department. Ho-Ho's™ were first hand-produced at Continental's San Francisco bakery in 1967. Equipment was later developed and placed around the country to allow for national distribution.

Ho-Ho's™ are a modified version of the European treat known as Swiss rolls. In 1970, Continental became the first national bakery to adopt open-dating of bread products and to introduce nutrition information on bread. Hostess O's™ were developed and introduced in 1973. In the eighties, Continental introduced Wonder Light™, a reduced calorie bread and the Hostess™ pudding line. In 1990, Continental began distribution of the Bread Du Jour™ product line and the Hostess Light™ product lines.

All trademarks and logos are the sole property of Continental™, Wonder™, and Hostess™. Our thanks to Jennette R. Bachmann of Continental Baking for the information furnished for this article.

Curtiss Candy
Chicago, Illinois

Just before World War I, Otto Schnering leased a small room over a plumber's shop in Chicago. He hired four employees and began to make candy. Although war provided a boost to his business, he still felt that he needed something to improve his line. He tried Curtiss ostrich eggs, Curtiss coconut grove, Curtiss milk loaf, Curtiss Peter Pan and a host of other product lines. Finally in 1920 he hit the jackpot with a caramel, nut, and chocolate bar.

Baby Ruth™ was not named for George Herman Ruth, "The Babe." Introduced in the early twenties, the name honors President and Mrs. Grover Cleveland's daughter who was referred to as "Baby Ruth." The trademark used on Baby Ruth™ was patterned exactly after the engraved lettering of the name used on a medallion struck for the Chicago World's Colombian Exposition in 1893. It pictured the President, his wife, and daughter, Baby Ruth. This product was the cornerstone of the candy empire that was known as Curtiss.

Butterfinger™, Curtiss' Candies second longest running hit, was introduced in 1928 and the name selected by public contest. The winning entry was a popular expression of the day used by sportscasters to describe athletes who were unable to hold on to a baseball or football. Predictably this was after the Chicago White Sox lost men like "Shoeless" Joe Jackson in the 1918 Black Sox's scandal. Jackson's glove was referred to as the place where triples went to die. Those that replaced the eight men out were by the standards of Chi town's sportswriters little more than "butterfingers."

Curtiss was an early giant and many distribution jars are found both for the entire Curtiss line, as well as for specific items. Among others, a standard Anchor Hocking one gallon and side loader with a white logo have turned up in the North and South Carolina region. The one gallon is by far the most common. A fully embossed jar without the pedestal was found in North Carolina and the pictured jar came from East Tennessee. The pedestal jar was patented by Curtiss to stop the use of Curtiss jars by competitors and is a fascinating answer to the problem of giving aid to the enemy.

Nabisco™ acquired Curtiss in the early sixties and Nestle acquired the surviving products in the 1990s. The Curtiss name is now sadly lost and only its surviving products are remembered. Today's Nestle™ "pitch men" have repeatedly shown their contempt for product history with Baby Ruth™ commercials that feature the wrong "Babe."

Butterfinger™, Baby Ruth™, Nestle™, and Nabisco™ are registered trademarks of the respective companies, where applicable trademarks and slogans are licensed, protected, and the sole property of those companies.

One gallon standard, white lettering, "Another Curtiss Product, Property of Curtiss Candy Co., Chicago, Illinois" — $25-$45.

 Another Curtiss Product

Property of Curtiss Candy Co., Chicago, Ill.

Logo from Standard Curtiss One Gallon Circular.

Curtiss One-Gallon, circa 1955.

Standard side-loader, white with Curtiss — $25-$45.

Another Curtiss Product

Property of
Curtiss Candy Co., Chicago, Ill.

Logo for Standard Curtiss flip lid side loader.

Variation of Standard Curtiss flip lid sideloader.

Curtiss Side Loader, circa 1955. *Ann S. Yarborough.*

Lid for Curtiss Chicos from Curtiss Patent Jar.

The Curtiss patented jar will only rest correctly on the patented tin advertising strip; Chico's Spanish Peanuts is the most common strip, with correct lid and strip for top value — $25-$125. This jar must be complete, with the lid and an advertising strip in excellent condition, with the shelf set at the bottom of the strip for top value.

CURTISS

5¢ CHICOS 5¢

SPANISH PEANUTS

Curtiss Chicos Strip from Curtiss Patent Jar.

Curtiss Chico's, Curtiss Patent Jar, circa 1925. *Ann S. Yarborough.*

Curtiss Chico's, Curtiss Patent Jar. *Ann S. Yarborough.*

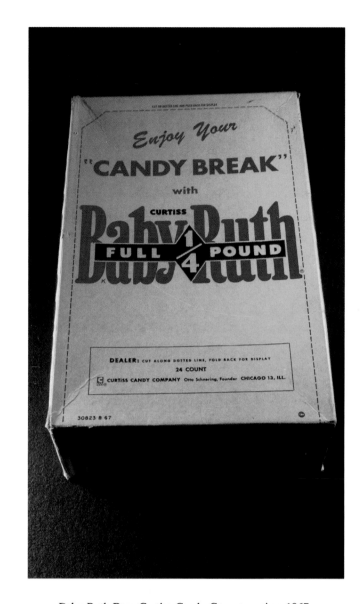

Baby Ruth Box, Curtiss Candy Company, circa 1967.

Lid, Curtiss Chico's, Curtiss Patent Jar. *Ann S. Yarborough.*

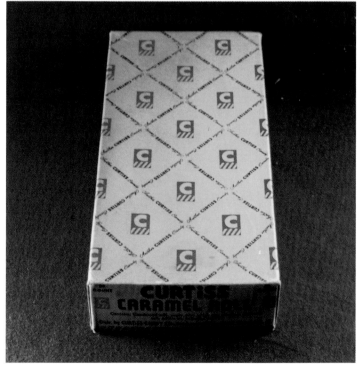

Curtiss Caramel Roll Box, circa 1957.

Dad's Cookies

Little is known about this company. One jar embossed Property of Dad's Cookies turned up in South Carolina. The jar is very large, probably three or four gallons. Judging by the glass, it is either fairly old or a crudely made product. Any information would be appreciated.

Three gallon, Property of Dad's Cookies — $35-$55.

PROPERTY OF DADS COOKIE CO.

Dad's logo as embossed on the large three-gallon jar.

Dad's Three Gallon Embossed, 1920-1945.

The standard two gallon jar, Dad's Cookies embossed in bottom, an illegible logo on the jar, with a very unusual red tin lid and finial. Value would probably be in the $35-$50 range with the correct lid and the logo intact.

Dad's logo as embossed in the bottom of the two gallon circular jar.

Dixie Biscuit Company
Atlanta, Georgia

Dixie was a large producer of cookies and crackers in the South. Little is known of its history but the Dixie Vanilla Cookie™ is still produced by Sunshine™ Biscuit Company. Sunshine™ can furnish no additional information and the Atlanta Public Library and Atlanta Chamber of Commerce are unable to help.

It is suspected that Dixie used a large number of jars of several types. The pictured jar was located in Greenville, South Carolina.

Red "Dixie" logo, "Atlanta, Ga." in blue, standard small cylinder — $40-$65.
Red "Dixie" logo, "Atlanta, Ga." in blue, standard large cylinder — $45-$75.

Dixie One Gallon, Atlanta, Georgia, circa 1955.

Atlanta, Georgia

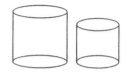

Dixie logo which features stars that are not shown.

Dixie cardboard potato chip container — $25-$35.

Dixie Potato Chip Canister, Atlanta, Georgia, circa 1960.

Elephant Peanuts

Elephant Peanuts used a potbelly jar with an embossed rampant elephant. This jar is very popular with country store collectors.

Fisher Nuts™
St. Paul, Minnesota
1920-

The Fisher Nut Company was established by a Russian immigrant following World War I. Sam Fisher served in France during the First World War and observed the French method of soaking the entire peanut in brine before roasting. Following the war he became the first in the United States to develop a process that was patented for salting nuts in the shell. Fisher marketed his product largely in major league ball parks. He expanded his business to include a full line of chocolate and nut products in the thirties and forties.

The company was known as Fisher's Nut and Chocolate Company from the late thirties through the early fifties. It became the Fisher Nut Company in the early fifties and was known as that until 1962.

During the fifties, Fisher™ developed the Tom Scott product line that was named for his grandson. All profits from that line were held in trust for the grand-children. From 1962 until 1984, the company was a subsidiary of Beatrice Foods™ and in 1989 was purchased by Proctor and Gamble™. The "s" was dropped from Fisher's around 1978.

Proctor and Gamble™ had no record of Fisher™ producing a composite peanut butter sandwich, but it would be a logical item to market with a peanut line. Proctor and Gamble™ are still working to fill in the blank spots in the history of Fisher Nuts.

Beatrice™, Proctor and Gamble™, and Fisher™ trademarks are the sole property of the respective companies. Thanks to Greg Perkins at Proctor and Gamble™ Corporate Archives for the information in this sketch.

Two-gallon Anchor-Hocking standard, Fishers™ Peanut Butter Sandwiches, red script. Probably dates from the 1950s, This jar was located in Horry County, South Carolina. Other examples of this jar have been seen in North Carolina and it is unconfirmed that this jar was used by Fisher Nut Company. The Fisher™ script is the same as the Fisher™ logo — $25-$50.

Fisher's
PEANUT BUTTER SANDWICHES

The Fisher logo as it appears on the two gallon jar is a red fired-on label.

Fisher's Two Gallon, circa 1955.

Frito-Lay
Plano, Texas
1961-
Frito 1932-1961
H.W. Lay Company 1938-1961

In 1932, Elmer Doolin paid one hundred dollars for the recipe of a corn chips snack and began the Frito Company in San Antonio, Texas. Shortly thereafter in 1938, Herman W. Lay established the H.W. Lay Company with the potato chip as its cornerstone product.

During early World War II, Lay's developed a method of production based on a continuous line potato chip machine. This was the first machine of its type and revolutionized the industry. In 1944, Lay's began advertisement on television when the Lay's character, Oscar, the happy potato, was introduced to the nation. Using this information, the change in shadowbox logos can be dated to around the end of World War II.

In 1945, the Frito Company granted the H.W. Lay Company exclusive franchise to manufacture and distribute Frito's corn chips in the Southeast, beginning a long and successful partnership. In the late forties, two hallmark events occurred at what would later become Frito-Lay. The Frito Company continued to expand its market with Cheeto's cheese-flavored snacks which were distributed by the Lay's Company and Frito's corn chips began an aggressive marketing campaign using the first national color advertising in magazines.

In the 1950s, an ever-expanding Frito-Lay made the following steps toward the realization of a national market. First Frito's introduced the Frito kid as the product representative and he appeared on the Dave Garroway Today show. The Ruffles product line was introduced in the late fifties to fill a particular market niche as packaging advances allowed for a longer shelf life. Vice-President Nixon took Nikita Krushchev a gift of Frito's corn chips, suggesting a sort of snack food détente that placed Frito's at the center of the nation's attention. Frito-Lay, with that move, positioned itself as the national snack food leader and vast rewards were earned in the coming decade.

In 1960, both Oscar and Lay's were linked with the Deputy Dawg Cartoon Show in a ground-breaking regional campaign. The next year the founder of Frito's, Elmer Doolin, died, after having seen his product grow from a one hundred dollar investment to a multi-million dollar company. This is also the year of the merger of H.W. Lay Company and Frito to form Frito-Lay Products Inc.

To respond to a changing national market, Frito-Lay examined its advertising and retired the Frito Kid in the late sixties. Lay's potato chips also chose a new advertising thrust with the new slogan, "Betcha can't eat just one."

In 1965, Lay's became the first regular potato chip to be marketed nationally. Two recent changes at Frito-Lay are worthy of note. The first was the acquisition of the west coast company, Grandma's Cookies. Grandma's was an established company that was founded in 1914 in the state of Washington. Second, in 1991, for the first time in 58 years, Frito's changed the packaging of its lead product, choosing brighter colors to appeal to a younger audience.

Frito-Lay continues to expand and grow as it faces the challenges of maintaining its identity in a large corporate body. Where applicable, trademarks and slogans are licensed, protected, and the sole property of Frito-Lay Inc. Thanks to Jan in consumer affairs at Frito-Lay. Much of the information was provided through her assistance. The jars and tins pictured were located in western North Carolina, eastern Tennessee, South Carolina, and Florida.

Lay's (Frito-Lay)
(Pre 1944-continued into the Fifties)

"Lay's shadow box logo" at top, 5 cents in center, "Go b-tween's" at bottom, standard large cylinder, red letters — $45-$65.

Lay's logo for standard two gallon and side-loader before "Oscar."

Lay's Shadowbox Logo: Two Gallon, circa 1946, prior to "Oscar."

"Lay's shadow box logo" at top, 5 cents in center, "Salted Peanuts" at bottom, standard small cylinder, red letters, (Post 1944 probably mid-fifties) — $35-$50.

Lay's logo for standard one gallon peanut Jar before "Oscar."

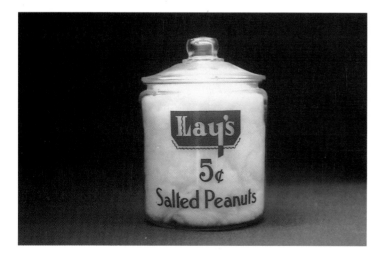

Lay's Shadowbox Logo: One Gallon, circa 1946, prior to "Oscar."

"Lay's shadow box logo" at top, 5 cents in center, "Go b-tween's" at bottom, standard side-loader, logo is white on both examples seen but probably faded too white. (The least common of the standard Lay's Jars.) — $65-$100.

Lay's Shadowbox Logo: Side Loader, circa 1946.

Oscar Versions

The year 1944 is the earliest possible date for use of this logo but it probably dates from the early to mid-fifties.

"Lay's" with "Oscar" potato head logo at top, 5 cents in center, "Go b-tween's" at bottom, standard large cylinder, red letters — $45-$65.

Lay's logos with "Oscar."

Lay's Oscar Logo: Two Gallon, circa 1955.

"Lay's" with "Oscar" potato head logo at top, 5 cents to side, "Salted Peanuts," at bottom, Frito-Lay logo in a red square, (post 1961), red letters standard small cylinder — $35-$50.

Lay's logos with "Oscar."

Lay's Oscar Logo: One Gallon, circa 1963 or later note Frito-Lay.

Tins

Lay's one pound tins, regardless of logo — $10-$35.

Lay's One Pound Potato Chip Tin with Oscar Logo, post World War II. The Oscar logo was adopted by Lay's in 1944, its use and inclusion on advertising was gradual. The transition to the new jar was gradual and probably did not start until well after World War II.

Lay's One Pound Potato Chip Tin with Oscar Logo. (Note the addition of the handle to the lid.)

Lay's three pound tins, regardless of logo — $25-$40.

Lay's Three Pound Tin, circa 1955.

Lay's one pound tin, paper label, 1950s vintage — $20-$40.

Lay's Yellow Utility Tin, the addition of FL indicates the tin post-dates the Frito-Lay merger, circa 1963. When the stylized letters FL are included in the Lay's logo, it indicates a date after 1961 when the official Frito-Lay merger was complete. This tin does not have the correct lid.

Lay's Shadowbox Logo: Two Gallon, Side Loader, One Gallon, circa 1945.

Lay's Oscar Logo: Two Gallon, 1950s, one pound tin (1950s), one gallon (1960s).

Lay's Red Utility Tin, no FL indicates it pre-dates the formal merger of the companies.

Goodest Foods
Abbeville, South Carolina

The story of Goodest Foods is so representative of the industry and the South of that time as to demand presentation. Faced with the changes forced on them by the Great Depression, this family sought a means of income that would support them in a world of panic. Gradually, they found the answer in the production of high quality snack products that could be marketed locally to ensure freshness and quality.

Goodest Foods became well-known in the outback that was South Carolina of the 1930s and 1940s. Goodest Foods was a family business located in Abbeville, South Carolina on a small farm. Initially potato chip production was in a one-room rented building. When the potato chip business outgrew the rented building, a new plant was built on farm property of the family of Elizabeth Callahan, one of the partners.

The other partner was Sarah Carwile, a cousin of Elizabeth. The plant was run by Hubert Crowther, Sarah's brother-in-law. The products were distributed by the ladies in Sarah's car that had the back seat removed.

Later they bought a delivery van for the purpose. The mainstay of Goodest Foods was its potato chip and peanut butter cracker line. The potato chips were prepared by and under the supervision of the sisters. Quality control was very strict and any defective chip was removed following each step, but particular attention was paid to chips following frying.

Mr. Benson C. McWhite relates that it was a joy to inspect chips, as one could eat all the defective chips found. Clip racks were purchased in Allendale, South Carolina and were manufactured by a small company in that town. Crackers were prepared with peanut butter also by and under the supervision of the sisters. The crackers were bought in bulk from the Lance™ cracker bakery in Charlotte. This was an early (1938) and logical expansion for Lance™ Inc.

Jars and clip racks were the normal methods of distribution for the packaged composite crackers. All the items in the Goodest line were hand-packaged and no broken chips or crackers left either production or packing. Everything possible was done to ensure quality packaging and freshness. The products were exchanged in the stores on a weekly basis. This information is provided by Benson C. "Mac" McWhite of Greenville, South Carolina, a well-loved and long-time employee of Milliken.

Golden Flake Company
Lakeview, Texas

The standard one and two gallon containers with Golden Flake in yellow letters across the front are the only containers encountered so far. Golden Flake has not responded to requests for information about the company and its history. These jars were located in western and middle Tennessee.

Golden Flake's logo in yellow and fired-on both the one and two gallon jars.

One gallon, yellow letters, Golden Flake — $25-$45.

Golden Flake: One Gallon, Texas, circa 1955.

Two gallon, yellow letters, Golden Flake — $40-$65.

Golden Flake: Two Gallon, Texas, circa 1955.

Gordon's™ Foods
Louisville, Kentucky

Single truck logo decal, jar embossed in the bottom — "Property of Gordon's Food Inc., Trucks serving the South, Not to be sold" — $60-$85.

Gordon's™ was owned by Sunshine Biscuit and sold to Highland Foods. It is now operating out of the same Louisville headquarters as an independent organization. Gordon's™ Foods has failed to reply to numerous inquiries about its history and distribution jars.

Gordon's™ little truck logo is an all-time favorite and one of the most quickly recognized and collectible containers. Gordon's™ tin lids are stamped Gordon's™. All are flat and have a wooden button finial. It is reported that some original tin lids are unstamped with a variety of finial styles. Glass replacements may have been used by Gordon's™ and an almost mythical "G" glass lid is reported.

The logo, "Trucks serving the South." does exist and is embossed in the bottom of one of the examples listed below. Original single truck logos usually have a matted appearance, rather dull and rough even when waxed.

The jars mentioned and pictured were located in Georgia, South Carolina, Tennessee, and Kentucky.

Gordon's™ was purchased by Sunshine Biscuit.

Other earlier jars

This illustration of the bottom of a standard one gallon jar shows an early Gordon's embossed jar. The jar bears a single decal with Gordon's Food Products in the panel of the little truck. This jar was purchased from an antique dealer from the Richmond area. This early version also appears under the truck in some cases.

Gordon's Foods Inc., Trucks Serving the South, One Gallon Embossed, circa 1942-45.

This truck panel is seen on a cardboard packing case used by Milton Bradley toys to ship Gordon's Stay Fresh Tins to the Atlanta Distributor. The box is marked Gordon's Foods Inc., Atlanta, Ga.

Gordon's One Gallon Decal Jar, Trucks Serving the South (upright view). The use of a decal appears to have been common in the 1940s and may have been brought on by the rationing restrictions of World War II. See the Lance section for a full discussion of the possibilities.

Bottom of the Gordon's "Truck's Serving the South," Jar.

Gordon's Single Truck Logo: One Gallon, circa 1945.

Single Truck Logo Jars

Single truck logo (? — Fifties), red letters, truck on one side, truck labeled, "Gordon's™ Fresh Foods, logo, "Trucks serving the best," standard large cylinder — $45-$85.

This Gordon's Food Products panel is found on a decal that was placed on the Gordon Foods Inc., Trucks Serving the South, one gallon jar. The panel is seen stenciled on the panel delivery.

Single truck logo (? — Fifties), red letters, truck on one side, truck labeled, "Gordon's™ Fresh Foods," logo, "Trucks serving the best," standard small cylinder — $35-$55. (This jar has been poorly duplicated, using current Anchor-Hocking standard jars, with a glass lid and a very bright logo.)

Gordon's Single Truck Logo: Two Gallon, circa 1945.

Double Truck Logo

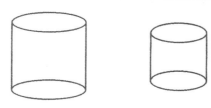

This Gordon's Fresh Foods Panel is found on the large single truck logo on both the standard Anchor-Hocking one and two gallon jars.

Gordon's Double Truck Logo: Two Gallon, circa 1955.

Double truck logo (fifties-sixties), red letters, truck on two sides, truck labeled, Gordon's™, logo "Trucks serving the best," standard small cylinder — $35-$55.

The plain Gordon's panel is found on the double truck logo one and two gallon jars. It is believed this is chronologically correct but no written confirmation is available. Gordon's jars used a marked metal lid with a wooden finial but it is possible glass lids were used as well.

Gordon's Steel Lids, two and one gallon lids.

Gordon's Double Truck Logo: One Gallon, circa 1955.

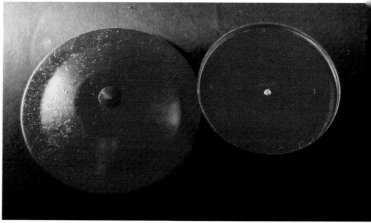

Double truck logo (fifties-sixties), red letters, truck on two sides, truck labeled, Gordon's™, logo "Trucks serving the best," standard large cylinder — $45-$85.

Plastic, Composite and Cardboard store containers

Gordon's had a plastic/composite store container much like the common Jack's and Murray containers with the tin lids. These are all a standard size and a little larger than the two gallon jar. This is usually seen with the Sunshine Biscuitman logo so it dates after the Sunshine buy-out — $25-$35.

Cardboard Potato Chip Container, dates after the Sunshine buy-out and lists other companies included in that buy-out, including Krun-chee — $20-$30.

Gordon's™ Tins

This little truck bears a panel marked Gordon's Fresh Potato Chips. It appears on both the one and three pound sizes of potato chips.

Gordon's™, one pound tin, without regard to variations of printing — $25-$50.

Gordon's Three Pound Tin, circa 1955.

Gordon's™, Stay Fresh Tin — small Gordon's™ truck for finial with stay-fresh crystals visible — tin is unmarked and usually carries instructions for proper use inside the lid — $25-$60.

Gordon's Stay Fresh Tin (top view), circa 1955.

Gordon's One Pound Tin, circa 1955.
Magicpak was used in the early 1960s.

Gordon's™, three pound tin, without regard to variations of printing — $25-$50.

Gordon's Stay Fresh Tin (side view), circa 1955.

Gordon's Stay Fresh Tin and the box used to ship tins from Milton Bradley to Atlanta, Georgia.

Gordon's™ Cardboard Containers with logo — $10-$25.

Close up of Gordon's Box Logo.

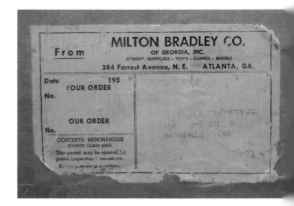

Close up of Label used on Gordon's Box.

Gordon's™ Kitchen Clocks are also known.

This little truck panel is found on Gordon's Nut Products. This marking is found on both packaging and clip racks.

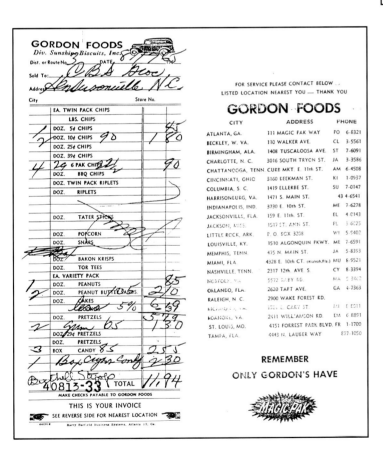

Gordon's receipts listing products and featuring distributor information on the rear. Note Magicpak logo, circa 1963.

Hyder Foods receipt, circa 1963.

Hershey Foods
1886-

Milton Hershey established the Lancaster Caramel Company in Lancaster, Pennsylvania in 1886. He brought with him to that factory a process for making caramel that he learned in Denver. This process was an improvement over anything available at the time and involved the use of fresh milk. The production of "Hershey Crystal A™" caramel netted him a fortune following many failures.

In 1895, following the Chicago Exposition, he began to manufacture the chocolate bars and cocoa products that would make him famous. By 1900, Hershey decided to concentrate on chocolate and sold the caramel company for one million dollars, retaining all rights and the equipment to manufacture his chocolate.

It would be several years before he perfected his process. In 1905, he built his new plant and began to mass produce the Hershey's milk chocolate bar™. Hershey believed in and practiced a paternalistic approach to business that was typical of the time in which he lived. Unlike others, Hershey totally "talked the talk and walked the walk."

In 1907, he introduced the Hershey's Kiss™ and chartered the Hershey Chocolate Company™ in 1908. With his money, he established the benevolent kingdom that still exists today. In 1925, the Mr. Goodbar™, another all time favorite, was introduced. Solid business practices and a great piece of lucky timing left Hershey better positioned for the depression than most companies and Mr. Hershey liked to say that Hershey's lost no employees during the era. However, he never accepted or understood the labor problems that beset his empire during this period.

In 1938, the company introduced the Krackel™ chocolate bar and then followed in 1939 with Hershey Miniatures™. During the Second World War, Hershey produced the dreaded D-bar. This was an all in one survival ration whose initiation no combat veteran missed. It provided 600 calories and would not melt. If the testimony of some veterans is to be believed it also could not be digested nor enjoyed no matter how creatively it was presented. Veterans have said that you could bury them and dig them up in ten-thousand years and they would taste just as bad. One gentleman stated that to this day he would not eat Hershey's milk chocolate as it reminded him of D-bars, and that is what death must taste like. All of this not withstanding, thousands who would have been hungry had a meal because of the D-bar and in many ways it may have been Hershey's greatest contribution to American history.

Post war expansion was good to the Hershey company but some stagnation occurred following his death. Beginning a new era in the late fifties, by 1963, Hershey's had consolidated its holdings. It began expansion by acquiring the H.B. Reese Candy Company and its line of products. As Mars pushed Hershey for leadership in the candy industry in the 1970s, the Hershey company decided to advertise for the first time in its long history. Further expansion came when an agreement was reached in 1970 with British candy maker Rowntree Mackintosh to distribute the Kit Kat™ wafer bar. In 1971, a second Rowntree Mackintosh product, the Rolo Caramel™, was introduced to the Hershey line. The Giant Hershey Kiss™ was introduced in 1978 and the Big Block™ candy line followed as did the premium candies in the Golden Line™. In 1986, Hershey acquired the Dietrich Corporation, the maker of the Fifth Avenue™ candy bar, Luden's throat drops, and Mello Mints™. Finally, in 1987, Hershey acquired from Nabisco, the Canadian operations of Life Savers, Planters and Lowney/Meirs chocolate.

In 1988, Hershey again became the big boy in the United States candy industry with the acquisition of distribution rights to Peter Paul/Cadbury, an American subsidiary of the British Cadbury Schweppes Company. With this deal Hershey gained the right to manufacture the Cadbury Company brands including Mounds™, Almond Joy™, York Peppermint Patties™, and Cadbury's specialty chocolates.

Hershey Foods	Date
Hershey's milk chocolate bars™	1905
Hershey's milk chocolate bars with almonds™	1907
Hershey's Kisses™	1907
Mr. Goodbar™	1925
Krackel™	1938
Hershey's miniatures™	1939

Hershey Kisses Box (side view), circa 1920.

Hershey Kisses Box (top view), circa 1920.

H.B. Reese Candy Company (acquired by Hershey 1963)

H.B. Reese was born in Pennsylvania in 1879. In 1917, he moved to Hershey, Pennsylvania. He entered the candy market with limited success with two products, Johnny Bars and Lizzie Bars. They were a caramel like molasses candy and a coconut candy. During the mid-1920s he developed a peanut butter cup to be included in assortments. Ten years later he developed a larger cup and sold them for a penny each.

Sugar shortages and rationing during the Second World War prompted Reese to discontinue all his other lines and concentrate on peanut butter cup production. Production and distribution were traditionally handled by jobbers, vending machines, and syndicated stores. Growth in the post war era was phenomenal. In 1957, a new plant was constructed in Hershey on Chocolate Avenue. Six years later, H.B. Reese Candy Company, Inc. was sold to Hershey. In 1976, Reese Crunchy™ was introduced. However, in 1991, this product was reformulated. The most recent marketing effort of the company is Reese's Peanut Butter. Today specialty items are also a part of the Reese line including pumpkins, eggs, and other seasonal items.

Hershey Kisses Box (end view), circa 1920.

Luden's
Reading, Pa.

In 1891, William H. Luden established his candy making business in Reading, Pennsylvania. This followed his apprenticeship with Koller & Barret, a Reading ice cream and confectionery manufacturer. This first business was established using a coal-burning stove in his mother's kitchen. The primary product of the company was "Moshie," a Pennsylvania Dutch treat made from corn syrup and brown sugar. First distributing on street corners, as the business grew Luden developed one of the first candy distribution systems in the nation, establishing distributors as middle men to handle sales in other cities and regions.

In 1900, Luden moved to its present site in Reading and was manufacturing over three million pounds of candy per year. His most famous creation was the amber-colored throat drop. Luden discovered that the essential ingredients used to make candies were the same as those used for throat drops. He developed a formula that would make the drops taste good and relieve throat irritations. After consultation with a local pharmacist, Luden began manufacturing the menthol throat drop. Traditionally marketed only in the color red, Luden changed the color to amber. Luden's also invented machinery to manufacture candy. His best known creation is a peanut-shelling device he created from the wringer of his mother's washing machine.

In 1927, Luden's was bought by the Dietrich family of Dietrich Inc. Dietrich Inc. was sold to Hershey in 1986. Luden also developed the Fifth Avenue™ candy bar that was first manufactured in 1936 for Dietrich Inc. Fifth Avenue™ and Mello-Mints™ were both acquired at this time.

Planters and Life Savers (Canada) were acquired by Hershey in 1987, see Planters. Hershey acquired the US rights to distribute Cadbury products in 1988.

Hershey acquired US rights, 1970-71, for the Rowntree Mcintosh Rolo and Kit Kat candies.

Luden's "Dakota Jar" by Tiffin glass — $250 + in excellent condition

Peter Paul
New Haven, Connecticut

Acquired by Cadbury-Schweppes in 1978, Peter Paul was formed in New Haven, Connecticut in 1919. The Peter Paul Mound™ was introduced in 1920, as a single bar selling for 5 cents. In 1929, Peter Paul, Inc. was formed as a Delaware Corporation and acquired Winters and Co. of Philadelphia. Also in that year, Peter Paul bought J.N. Collins Company, producers of Walnettos, Honey Scotch, and Butter Scotch caramels. In 1932, the bar size of the Mound was doubled and the price held at a nickel. As a result of this move sales increased dramatically.

In 1947, the Almond Joy™ was introduced as a double bar with a dime price. Almond Joy sales did well in spite of the prevailing nickel price for candy. In 1948, Peter Paul raised the price of the Mound to a dime. In 1965, in an attempt to expand market size Peter Paul introduced the Caravelle. In 1966, the Walter H. Johnson Candy Company, maker of Powerhouse bars,

was acquired by Peter Paul. Bachman chocolate manufacturing company became a part of the Peter Paul family in 1968.

Continuing to expand, Peter Paul bought the Delicious Cookie Company in 1970 and the York Cone Company, makers of York Peppermint Patties™. By 1973, the prevailing price of all candy was a dime and increased pressure due to commodity cost forced a price increase to fifteen cents. Peter Paul changed from chocolate to a high grade confectioner's coating for Mounds and Almonds Joy in the same year. In 1975, the Almond Joy changed from two nuts to one nut per piece but in 1976, both candies returned to the chocolate covering. The milk chocolate Mound was introduced in 1976 and in 1978 Cadbury and Peter Paul merged.

Peter Paul Mounds, circa 1933-1947.

Peter Paul Mounds, circa 1933-1947.

Peter Paul Mounds Box (top view), circa 1950.

Peter Paul Mounds Box (side view), circa 1950.

Peter Paul Almond Joy Box (top view), circa 1950.

Peter Paul Almond Joy Box (side view), circa 1950.

Peter Paul Mounds, circa 1965.

Peter Paul Chiffon, circa 1965.

York Cone Co.

In 1972, the York Cone Company, maker of York Peppermint Patties was acquired by Peter Paul. Distribution was concentrated in six states. The next year Peter Paul moved to Food Brokers Sales Force and consolidated York as a Peter Paul brand. In 1975, York was expanded to coast to coast distribution.

Y & S Candies
Brooklyn, N.Y.

Acquired by Hershey in 1978, Y & S Candies was founded in Brooklyn, New York in 1845 by J.S. Young and C.A. Smylie. Y & S merged with H.W. Petherbridge and Scudder Bros. (F.P and F.V. Scudder) Licorice Makers in 1902 to form the National Licorice Company. National Licorice maintained Y & S as the trademark. Within months of the merger, National (Y & S) bought several other companies and issued stock to finance a new plant located in Brooklyn. Today four plants are currently in production. They are in Lancaster, Pennsylvania, Moline, Illinois, Farmington, New Mexico, and Montreal, Canada. The name was changed to Y & S Candies in 1968. In 1977, Hershey acquired Y & S Candies.

Y & S embossed jar with screw on lid — $25- $35.
Y&S see-through tin — $35-$50.
Hershey's candy company — 1993 Christmas jar — standard Anchor-Hocking small — $25.

Hershey Jar, circa 1990.

Hiland Foods
Des Moines, Iowa
1917-

Hiland Foods began during World War I when an elderly couple started making donuts in their kitchen and selling them door-to-door in the Highland Park area of Des Moines. After the war the couple sold the business to a veteran, William Alexander. Mr. Alexander and his spouse continued to make donuts and added potato chips to the line. Grocers began asking to carry the products, and Mr. Alexander purchased a truck and hired a driver to meet the demand. In 1926 the business was purchased by Mr. Art Holman.

Mr. Holman received for his investment two coal stoves, two 24 inch kettles, a hand slicer, and a Gem hand-crank donut machine. He supplemented the seasonal business by manufacturing chili in bricks and selling it during the winter. Holman and Alexander sold the business back and forth until January of 1929 when Holman emerged with the business. Expansion had been good during these years, for in 1929 Hiland boasted two shop girls, a driver, and a 200 square foot building. In 1931 Mr. Holman added egg noodles and horseradish to the line and replaced the coal stoves with gas-fired kettles that could fry 100 pound of potatoes an hour. In 1933 he again expanded and installed the first automatic potato chip machine to be delivered west of the Mississippi. In 1936 a new partner, Roy Murray, was acquired and a new plant constructed in Davenport. Within two years a larger location was required.

Hiland continued to expand until the death of Mr. Holman in 1961. Mr. Murray acquired the Davenport operation, and the Iowa Investment and Mortgage Co. bought the Des Moines operation. In 1965 Hiland acquired Polly Parrot Potato Chip of Sioux Falls, South Dakota. Finally in 1978 Hiland Des Moines acquired the Davenport plant from Roy Murray's brother. In 1979 all operations were merged into Hiland of Des Moines. Hiland acquired Old Vienna of St. Louis and both operations were absorbed by Curtice-Burns foods in 1988. Hiland was using a Scottish motif on its one pound tins in 1951 and probably followed other potato chip companies in packaging and marketing trends.

Hirsch's Goodies

The lid of this jar is very ornate; this information is furnished courtesy of the collection of Ann S. Yarborough. Information about this jar itself and the company is sought.

Jack's Cookies

Jack's used several plastic or composite containers. The early container is in blue and yellow and the later bears an orange and white logo. Jack's had other containers. These containers are often seen in the $10-$25 range.

Jack's Penny Cookie Plastic Jar, circa 1957.

43

Jack's Plastic Container, circa 1965.

EVERYTHING'S JAKE

JAKE'S

SALTED PEANUTS

PEANUT BUTTER SANDWICHES

BRENNON FOOD PRODUCTS CO. ATLANTA GEORGIA

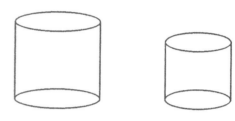

Jake's logo as it appears on both the one and two gallon jar.

One gallon standard, Everything's Jake, Jake's Salted Peanuts, Peanut Butter Sandwiches, Manufactured by Brennon Food Products Co., Atlanta, Ga. — $25-$45.

JACK'S COOKIE CORP.

Branch # 1 Route # 6 Date 7-1-63
Sold To C.B.S. Gro.
Store No.

Qty.	Unit	ITEM	AMOUNT	Qty.	Unit	ITEM	AMOUNT
	Box 1.55	2/1¢ C'nut Bar				SUB-TOTAL	
	Box 1.55	2/1¢ Ginger			Doz 1.44	15¢ Animal	
	Box 1.55	2/1¢ Tea					
	Box 1.55	2/1¢ Golden			Doz 2.76	29¢ Van. Waf. Bag	
	Box 1.80	2/1¢ Van. Waf.			Doz 2.76	29¢ Van. Waf. Box	
	Box	2/1¢ Choc. Chip			Doz 2.76	29¢ Sugar Waf.	
					Doz 2.76	29¢ Fig Bar	
	Box 1.80	1¢ C'nut Mac.		1	Doz 2.76	29¢ Creme Waf.	23
	Box	1¢ Ban. Creme					
	Box	1¢ Duplex Creme		3	Doz 3.72	39¢ Asstd.	94
	Box 1.80	1¢ Happy Jack			Doz 3.72	39¢ Choc. Chip	
	Box	1¢ Stage Plank			Doz 3.72	39¢ C'nut Mac.	
					Doz 3.72	39¢ Choc-Lite	
	Ctn .60	5¢ Choc. Pie			Doz 3.72	39¢ Lem. Creme	
	Ctn .60	5¢ Straw. Pie			Doz 3.72	39¢ Coco Creme	
	Ctn .60	5¢ Ban. Pie			Doz 3.72	39¢ Apple Betty	
	Doz .48	5¢ Poor Boy			Doz 3.72	39¢ Bon Bon	
	Doz .48	5¢ Rock & Roll			Doz 3.72	39¢ Banana	
					Doz 3.72	39¢ Oatmeal	
	Doz .96	10¢ Duplex			Doz 3.72	39¢ Pecan	
	Doz .96	10¢ Cocoa					
	Doz .96	10¢ Banana			Doz 4.70	49¢ Devils Food	
	Doz .96	10¢ Fig Bar					
		SUB-TOTAL					
						GROSS	1 17
		CUSTOMER'S SIGNATURE				RETURNS	
						DISCOUNTS	
15	(Stamp)					NET SALES	

THE SHELBY SALESBOOK CO., SHELBY, OHIO 56△484

JACK'S COOKIE CORP.

Branch # 1 Route # 6 Date 7-5-63
Sold To C.B.S. Gro.
Store No.

Qty.	Unit	ITEM	AMOUNT	Qty.	Unit	ITEM	AMOUNT
	Box 1.55	2/1¢ C'nut Bar				SUB-TOTAL	
	Box 1.55	2/1¢ Ginger			Doz 1.44	15¢ Animal	
	Box 1.55	2/1¢ Tea					
	Box 1.55	2/1¢ Golden		2	Doz 2.76	29¢ Van. Waf. Bag	46
	Box 1.80	2/1¢ Van. Waf.			Doz 2.76	29¢ Van. Waf. Box	
	Box	2/1¢ Choc. Chip			Doz 2.76	29¢ Sugar Waf.	
					Doz 2.76	29¢ Fig Bar	
	Box 1.80	1¢ C'nut Mac.			Doz 2.76	29¢ Creme Waf.	
	Box	1¢ Ban. Creme					
	Box	1¢ Duplex Creme			Doz 3.72	39¢ Asstd.	
	Box 1.80	1¢ Happy Jack			Doz 3.72	39¢ Choc. Chip	
	Box	1¢ Stage Plank			Doz 3.72	39¢ C'nut Mac.	
					Doz 3.72	39¢ Choc-Lite	
	Ctn .60	5¢ Choc. Pie			Doz 3.72	39¢ Lem. Creme	
	Ctn .60	5¢ Straw. Pie			Doz 3.72	39¢ Coco Creme	
	Ctn .60	5¢ Ban. Pie			Doz 3.72	39¢ Apple Betty	
	Doz .48	5¢ Poor Boy		4	Doz 3.72	39¢ Bon Bon	1 25
	Doz .48	5¢ Rock & Roll			Doz 3.72	39¢ Banana	
					Doz 3.72	39¢ Oatmeal	
	Doz .96	10¢ Duplex			Doz 3.72	39¢ Pecan	
	Doz .96	10¢ Cocoa					
	Doz .96	10¢ Banana			Doz 4.70	49¢ Devils Food	
	Doz .96	10¢ Fig Bar					
		SUB-TOTAL					
						GROSS	1 71
		CUSTOMER'S SIGNATURE				RETURNS	
						DISCOUNTS	
22	(Stamp)					NET SALES	

THE SHELBY SALESBOOK CO., SHELBY, OHIO 56△484

Jack's Products receipt, circa 1963.

Jake's Peanuts
Brennon Foods
Atlanta, Georgia

Jake's produced both a one and a two gallon jar that appear to be from the 1950s or 1960s. I have been unable to locate

Jake's: One Gallon, circa 1955.

Two gallon standard, Everything's Jake, Jake's Salted Peanuts, Peanut Butter Sandwiches, Manufactured by Brennon Food Products Co., Atlanta, Ga. — $40-$65.

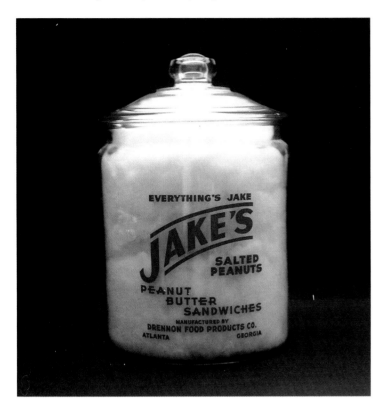

Jake's: Two Gallon, circa 1955.

One pound Jake's Potato Chip Tin — $10-$25.

Jake's: One Pound Tin, circa 1955.

Johnson Bakery
Milwaukee, Wisconsin

Brass Front/Glass Front Tin Blue and White logo — $55-$75.

Johnson Box Covers, Nickel and glass — $15-$25.

Keebler Biscuit Company
1853-

Keebler was founded in Philadelphia in 1853. It is suspected that it was not founded by elves, but the information provided by Keebler does not confirm or deny the possibility.

On November 3, 1927, the United Biscuit Company of America was incorporated with the joining of the Sawyer Biscuit Company, the Strietmann Biscuit Company of Cincinnati, the Union Biscuit Company of St. Louis, the Felber Biscuit Company of Columbus, Ohio, the Lakeside Biscuit Company, of Toledo, the Manchester-Sioux Falls Biscuit Company of Fargo and Sioux Falls, the Merchants (Bowman) Biscuit Company of Denver, and the Chicago Carton Company of Chicago.

In 1929 the United Biscuit Company of America acquired the Keebler-Weyl Biscuit Company of Philadelphia, The Purity Biscuit Company of Salt Lake City, and the Tennessee Biscuit Company of Nashville. Tennessee Biscuit was also known as the Belle-Meade Biscuit Company but the name change was made later.

This parent company was to continue to acquire properties in a de-centralized organization until 1966 when the name United Biscuit Company was changed to Keebler. Centralization was primarily between the end of World War II and 1966. In 1938 the manufacturing subsidiaries became divisions of the parent company and the current Philadelphia plant of the Keebler-Weyl Baking Division was completed. In 1941 the Iten-Barmettler Biscuit Company was acquired as was the Merchants Biscuit Division of Omaha. In 1942 the Cincinnati Plant of Strietmann was completed. In 1944 the Mac Sim Bar Paper Company became a subsidiary of the United Biscuit Company. In 1947 all assets of the paper company were bought by Keebler. In 1948 the name of the Merchants Biscuit Division of Denver was changed to the Bowman Biscuit Division. In 1949 post-war expansion allowed the completion of the Grand Rapids Plant of the Hekman Biscuit Division. Further consolidation resulted in the closure of the Lakeside Biscuit Division in Toledo. The change of the name of the Tennessee Biscuit Division in Nashville to the Belle-Meade Biscuit Division was made in 1951. The Quality Biscuit Division of Milwaukee was closed in 1952.

The process of consolidation led to a name change of the Keebler-Weyl Division to the Keebler Biscuit Division and the changing of the Ontario Biscuit Division in Buffalo to the Keebler Biscuit Division, Buffalo. Expansion of the Keebler Company in the fifties would continue to reflect the boom times of post-World War II. In 1953 Keebler opened the Melrose Park Plant of the Sawyer Biscuit Division. In 1954 Keebler expanded into the Deep South with the completion of a new plant by the Strietmann Division in Macon, Georgia. The older facilities were closed including Felber Biscuit Division of Columbus, The Colonial Biscuit Division of Pittsburgh, and the Union Biscuit Division in St. Louis. The production facility at Buffalo closed in 1956, but the sales division in that city continued. In 1957 the Old World Baking Division in Michigan City was founded. The new Bowman Biscuit Division plant in Denver was begun in 1959 and the Belle-Meade Division of Nashville was closed. Growing into the new decade, the Manchester Biscuit Division of Sioux Falls, the Keebler Division in Buffalo, the Manchester Biscuit Division in Fargo, and the Purity Biscuit Division in Salt Lake City were all closed and the Chicago Carton Division and the Mac Sim Bar Paper Division were sold to Waldorf Paper Products in 1960.

In 1961, Keebler completed the unification program and opened a new plant in Denver. Closings and acquisitions continued into the 1960s with the termination of manufacturing at Merchants Biscuit Division in Omaha in 1962 and the acquisition of Meadors, Inc., a candy company in Greenville, South Carolina in 1963.

In 1962 Keebler also announced a new brand-mark, that of Supreme Kitchen Rich. In 1963 Keebler also acquired all the assets of the Old World Baking Company in Michigan City. In 1965 Keebler acquired the assets of the Illinois Baking Corporation of Chicago and sold the Melrose Park Plant to Zenith. Manufacturing was concluded at the Supreme-Melrose Park Bakery in the next year. Also in 1966 the name of United Biscuit was changed to Keebler and the corporate offices moved to Elmhurst, Illinois.

The elves are apparently much more interested in baking than promotion or history as Keebler has no information past the mid-sixties. It is to their credit that in failing to update their history, the elves have accidentally preserved it in an unedited format so that the origin of the company is easy to trace.

Keebler and the elves are registered trademarks of the Keebler Company, where applicable, trademarks and slogans are licensed, protected, and the sole property of the companies.

Ray Klug, in his *Antique Advertising Encyclopedia* (ISBN 0-89145-259-1), shows an excellent example of a Strietmann glass front tin, not unlike the Nabisco item pictured in that section. Since distribution methods are usually regional, I would date this between 1880-1920. Klug's pioneering works on advertising are included by every collector as necessary in a good resource library.

Value would be between $35-$55 on a brass front Strietmann Tin.

Keebler-Weyl wooden biscuit boxes with labels intact — $35-$75.

Tennessee Biscuit had a half-sized glass and brass front tin that normally sells for $25- $50.

Keebler Company

Company Name	Formed	Joined	Closed
Belle-Meade or Tennessee Biscuit Changed to Belle-Meade (1951), Nashville, Tennessee		1915	1959
Bowman Biscuit Co. Denver, Colorado	1905	1927	
Colonial Biscuit Co. Pittsburgh, Pa.	1905	1928	1954
Felber Biscuit Co. Columbus, Ohio	1875	1927	1954
Hekman Biscuit Co. Grand Rapids, Iowa	1893	1928	1949
Illinois Baking Co.		1931	1965
Iten-Barmettler Biscuit Co. Joined Merchants	1941		
Keebler - Weyl Biscuit Co. Keebler - Weyl name Changed to Keebler (1952) Philadelphia, Pa. Buffalo, N.Y. plant closed 1956	1853		1929
Lakeside Biscuit Co. Toledo, Ohio	1901	1925	1951
Manchester-Sioux Falls Bis. Co. Fargo and Sioux Falls, S.D. Manchester-Fargo Biscuit Co.	1902	1927	1960
Meadors Inc. Greenville, S.C.	1919		1963
Merchants Biscuit Company Omaha, Ne.		1931	1962
Old World Baking Michigan City, Michigan.		1957	1963
Ontario Biscuit Co. Changed to Keebler name (1953) Buffalo, N.Y.		1903	1928
Purity Biscuit Co. Salt Lake City, Utah	1915	1929	1960
Quality Biscuit Co. Milwaukee, WI.	1952		
Sawyer Biscuit Co. Changed name to Sawyer from Melrose Park Supreme (1960)	1901	1925	1953
Strietmann Biscuit Co. Cincinnati, Ohio	1856	1927	
Supreme Bakers Melrose Park See Sawyer Biscuit Co.	1901	1925	1966
Tennessee Biscuit Co. Nashville, TN. (See Belle-Meade)	1915	1929	
Union Biscuit Co. St. Louis, Mo.	1899	1925	1954

These units were divested as opposed to being closed.

Company Name	Formed	Joined	Closed
Chicago Carton Company Chicago, IL.	1908	1960	
Mac Sim Bar Paper	1905	1944	1960

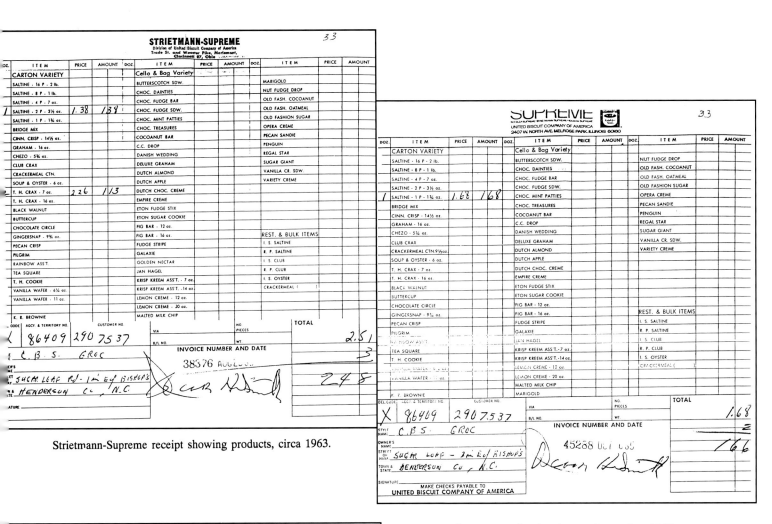

Strietmann-Supreme receipt showing products, circa 1963.

Supreme receipt showing products, circa 1965.

Strietmann receipt showing products, circa 1963.

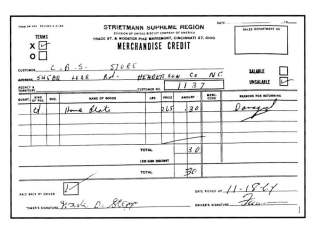

Strietmann-Supreme Credit Voucher, circa 1964.

Lance™ Packing Company
Lance™ Inc.
Lance™
1912-
Charlotte, North Carolina

Lance™ Packing Company first appeared in the Charlotte, North Carolina, telephone book in 1913.[1] Company reports date the founding as 1912.[2] The company, founded by Mr. P.L. Lance and Mr. Salem A. Van Every, began as a food brokerage dealing mainly in coffee. Many items were packaged under the Lance™ logo but peanut products became the mainstay of the Lance™ line. Company legend states that Mr. Lance was left "holding the bag" on a 500 pound peanut deal gone bad. Rather than suffer the loss, Mr. Lance took the peanuts home, roasted them, and peddled them for five cents a bag on the streets of Charlotte.[3] It would be difficult to imagine Mr. Lance or Mr. Van Every peddling peanuts, but the legend persists and is probably closer to fact than we can imagine as we approach the twenty-first century.

Armed with assets of sixty dollars, Mr. Lance installed a peanut roaster and a peanut butter mill on the second floor of 204 South College Street in Charlotte. The business moved from a family kitchen to a business address. Mr. Lance packed and sold peanut butter and peanuts, as well as other products, for local merchants to distribute.[4] Coffee packaging from these early years would be especially interesting to the collector.

Early in the life of the company, Mr. Lance moved ahead with an idea of his wife's for spreading peanut butter on crackers. This was a more productive use for the company's peanut butter and Mr. Lance created the composition sandwich.[5] Lance™ believes this was the first attempt to market the "combination sandwich" in America.[6]

Soldiers on the move have always been a source of revenue to the communities in which they serve and like Duke's Sandwich and Mayonnaise Co. of Greenville, South Carolina, Lance™ too, owes a debt of gratitude to the doughboy. During World War I, a soldier at Camp Greene gave the partners at Lance™ a recipe for the popular piece of candy which today is called the peanut bar. The bar was packed in empty shirt boxes saved by downtown merchants and was the company's first venture into candy production.[7]

Shortly before America became involved in the First World War, Lance™ distributed a beautifully embossed candy jar.[8] This jar was given in hard candy deals from 1916 through the 1920s. It is commonly called the Lance™ Apothecary Jar and carries a fitted ground lid. Around 1919, a companion sandwich jar was introduced. The sandwich jar is often referred to as The Ginger Jar or the Acorn Jar.[9] In the early 1920s, an octagonal jar with a teardrop finial was used by Lance™ distributors. This jar carried the Lance™ Packing Company logo embossed above a circle with crossed lances inside the circle. This appeared above the words, Charlotte, N.C.

In the mid-twenties, the ball or basketball jar was introduced with the "Insist on Lance's™" logo in red letters flanked by one lance on either side of the logo.[10] This is reported in blue but the red is confirmed. This jar was made by either several different glass companies or one glass company that changed lid types during production. These jars were widely used and are found in two sizes. This logo would be one of the easiest to duplicate, so care should be taken in the purchase of these jars.[11]

A blue "INSIST ON LANCE'S" logo was used on a standard Anchor-Hocking circular one-gallon jar and a side-loading standard jar that had a complex closure system for the lid.[12] This logo also appears on the standard octagonal jar.[13] These jars are dated by some sources as from the early 1930s, specifically 1932. The delicate finial is the correct lid for the circular one-gallon jar but Lance™, like any other company, would certainly have used existing inventory to replace lids on later jars. These jars were used through the growth of the late 1920s and early 1930s and this is the most common logo used in the early years. The logo would be easy to duplicate so care should be taken to view known examples before purchase.

The company moved to 1300 South Boulevard in 1926. Mr. Lance, the founder and namesake of the company, was killed in an automobile accident in that year and Mr. Van Every assumed leadership. By 1935, Lance™ had reached the million dollar mark in sales and in 1938 Lance™ began the manufacture of crackers.[14] These were distributed to smaller companies in five and ten pound containers and these companies then produced composition sandwiches under their logo. Goodest Foods of Abbeville, South Carolina, was one such small company.[15]

In 1939, Lance™ reached two million dollars in sales and the company incorporated. The name was changed to Lance™ Inc. but the use of Lance™ Inc. on logos may predate 1939. However, the target or seal logo can be found with both Lance™ Inc. and Lance™ Packing Company used as the company name.[16]

This time of explosive growth between 1935 and 1945 brought many changes in jars and company logos. This is the era that introduced the decal jars. They appear around 1938. A standard octagonal jar, the one gallon circular and the pretzel or paneled candy jar are all found with Lance™ decals.[17] The one-gallon circular is also found with Lance™ Packing Company, Charlotte, N. Car. embossed in the bottom and a decal.[18] The logo that consisted of the word, Lance™, in red over blue crossed lances was also introduced, and examples of circular jars bearing this logo are known.[19] The Lance™ Packing Products octagon and the "big bottom" standard Sandwich and Barber Jars also date from this time.

One can speculate about the appearance of these jars and the changes in distribution caused by explosive growth during the depression and a wartime economy, but little is known beyond speculation. Was the use of the decal and many logos brought on by explosive growth of the late thirties or was it the result of wartime rationing? This author feels that a reasonable explanation for the use of something as delicate as a decal on a jar would be wartime rationing or vast growth, others feel it was simply a matter of cost effectiveness. All three explanations are logical and rational and the truth may be a combination of all three. However, why that decal would say Lance™ Packing Company instead of Lance™ Inc. cannot be explained, unless the decals were drawn from the existing stock that pre-dates 1939. This could also have been a method used to increase sales with a jar "give away." Lance™ was extremely creative in meeting market needs both during and before the war. It was a lean, mean sales machine during both eras. Purchase of over-stocked items produced by glass companies in the thirties would be typical of the highly adaptable management of Lance™ during these years but no confirmation of this exists. What is known is that Lance™ continued to grow and used every means possible to spur that growth.

World War II brought vast changes in the Lance™ Company. Sugar was scarce during the war and the decision was made to de-emphasize candies and concentrate on the peanut products. The Lance™ Company was called upon to produce special packaging for shipping items overseas. Lance™ also produced specialized tools for the war effort.[20] As manpower was critical in the Charlotte area, a small operation was set up in Rock Hill, South Carolina, to provide the needed services. It is believed that the Rock Hill operation also kept Lance™ supplied with the items needed to continue packing and shipping in tin. Certainly tins of all types that meet government specifications for packing food items are found with Lance™ Inc. labels. This causes one to speculate that these were produced just across the South Carolina state line in Rock Hill.

Lance™ lost many valuable employees to military service. In 1943, Mr. Van Every died and his son, Phillip Lance Van Every, assumed leadership of the Lance™ Company. Following World War II, Mr. Van Every began an aggressive marketing campaign. Under his leadership, vast new markets were opened and maintained. From 1950 to 1960, sales grew from fourteen million dollars to twenty-six million.[21] In 1953, the familiar red Lance™ over blue crossed lances were replaced by the pennant logo.[22] By 1960, Lance™ had outgrown its plant. In 1962, Lance™ moved operations to the current location.[23]

The sixties and seventies marked important changes at Lance™ in marketing and marketing strategy. The expanding economy demanded the death of the five-cent item. In a South that was suffering from the tremendous effects of change, the death of the "nickel lunch" was met with extreme resistance.[24] In 1967, Lance™ met this challenge head-on and redesigned its two jars to accommodate the new flat-pack of six crackers.[25] Competition was fierce in the Charlotte market with two other local companies of regional stature competing for customers.[26] The national market was no better, but the Lance™ strategy again proved to be the correct one, so that today few people remember the competition. On March 6, 1970 the last five-cent item left the Lance™ line.[27] Then in 1978, Lance™ produced its last jar and jar rack.[28] Vending machines had finally buried the once proud Lance™ distribution jar.

The "House of Lance™" continues its growth into the nineties, meeting all challenges with the same positive attitude that has brought it success through the years. For additional information the address of the Lance™ Company is Lance™ Inc., Box 32308, Charlotte, N.C. 28292. Where applicable, trademarks and slogans are licensed, protected, and the sole property of Lance™, Inc.

Lance™ Jars, Prior to 1920 and the Early 1920s

Lance™ slender candy jar, embossed, "Lance™ Packing Company, Charlotte, N.C.," price determined by market and condition — $250+ for no chips and undamaged.

First *Lance* Candy or Apothecary Jar (1916) and First *Lance* Sandwich, Acorn or Ginger Jar (1919).

Lance Apothecary Jar, 1916. See the Lance Apothecary Lid that follows. *Leon Helms.*

First Lance Jar, circa 1916. *Leon Helms.*

This logo was the first used by the *Lance Packing Company* on distribution jars. It appeared on the slender candy jar before 1920. The Sandwich Jar also used this logo. The Sandwich Jar is also known as The Ginger Jar or the Acorn Jar. The logo is always embossed.

49

Acorn Lid for the Ginger or Acorn Jar, 1919.

Lid from the Lance Apothecary Jar. *Leon Helms.*

Lance™ acorn or ginger jar, embossed, "Lance™ Packing Company, Charlotte, N.C.," price determined by market and condition — $200+ for no chips and undamaged.

Lance Acorn or Ginger Jar, 1919. The correct lid for this jar and the Squirrel Jar is the acorn lid, 1919.

Lance first Sandwich, Acorn, or Ginger Jar, circa 1919. *Leon Helms.*

Lance™ octagonal sandwich jar, embossed, "Lance™ Packing Company, Charlotte, N.C.," with crossed lances embossed inside a circle, price determined by market and condition — $150+ for no chips and undamaged.

Lance Acorn or first Sandwich Jar.

Lance Packing Company, Charlotte, North Carolina, Embossed Octagon, early 1920s. The correct lid for this jar is the Tear-Drop Finial Lid used for all standard octagonal jars dating prior to 1940.

Lance™ Jars, Early- to Mid-Twenties

This logo appears on the first octagonal jar used by Lance. It is embossed on a single side of the jar and covers three panels. This jar is often referred to as the Second Sandwich Jar. It was probably introduced in the early 1920s but there is no confirmation of this. Certainly by the late 1920s the *"Insist on Lance's"* blue logo was in use.

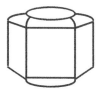

Standard Octagonal Jar.

Lance Packing Company, Charlotte, North Carolina, Embossed Octagon. The correct lid for this jar is also the Tear-Drop Finial Lid. Note the Lance Packing Stick Candy Box inside the jar. *Leon Helms.*

51

Tear-Drop Finial Lid used for many Standard Octagonal Jars prior to 1940.

Lance Packing Company, Charlotte, North Carolina, standard embossed Octagonal Jar, early 1920s. *Leon Helms.*

Lance™ Jars Mid-Twenties to Early-Thirties

These jars would be easy to reproduce and unmarked jars with correct lids are common. These facts keep the prices from inflating and will continue to do so.

Insist on Lance's™ Logo

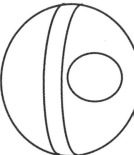

This logo in red appeared on the Ball or Basketball Jar. This logo and the jar are from the mid-to-late 1920s. The *"Insist on Lance's"* logo would be one of the easiest to duplicate and should always be examined with care. This jar is reported in blue but this is unconfirmed.

The Basketball or Ball Jar as viewed from above. The *"Insist on Lance's"* logo would appear in the raised ridge in the center. This jar is also seen in two sizes, the normal gallon jar and a smaller version. This jar is dated as appearing around 1926.

Lance™ ball or basketball jar with tin lid, "Insist on Lance™'s" flanked by a single lance in red or orange, more correctly. Lids were tin and are often missing — $150 for no chips and undamaged with lid.

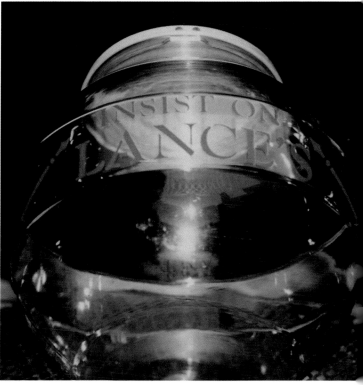

Insist on Lance's, Ball Jar, mid-1920s. *Leon Helms.*

Small and Large Ball Jar, mid-1920s. *Leon Helms.*

Insist on Lance's, Octagonal Jar, late 1920s/early 1930s. The correct lid for this jar is the Tear-Drop Finial Lid for most Standard Octagonal Jars prior to 1940.

Lance™ circular one gallon, "Insist on Lance's™" over crossed blue lances — $125 for no chips and undamaged, delicate finial lid is correct.

INSIST ON LANCE'S

This logo is found on both the octagonal and the one gallon circular jars produced in the late 1920s and early 1930s. The letters and the lances are in blue. This logo would be among the easiest to duplicate and is by far the most common.

Insist on Lance's, Octagonal Jar and One Gallon Circular Jar, late 1920s. The Acorn Lid on the circular jar is acceptable as a replacement. The jar was probably shipped with the delicate finial lid seen on other Lance circular one-gallon jars. *Leon Helms.*

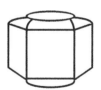 Standard Octagonal Jar.

 Standard Side Loader.

 Standard One gallon circular jar.

Lance™ octagonal jar, "Insist on Lance's™" over crossed blue lances — $150 for no chips and undamaged, slight premium with correct lid.

Lance™ side loader with complex closure system, "Insist on Lance's™ " over crossed blue lances — $150 for no chips and undamaged, premium for correct lid.

Lance Side Loader, circa 1932. *Leon Helms.*

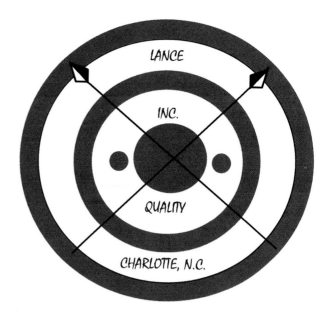

In 1939, the *Lance* company was incorporated and this logo was adopted. It is seen as a target and a seal. It may have been used before 1939 and certainly appears with *Lance Packing Company* instead of *Lance Inc.* It was used during World War II. The logo appears as a secondary logo on boxes produced in the late 1940s. The *Lance Packing Company* version of this logo is seen as a decal on the octagonal and the paneled candy jar and the one gallon jar. It is also seen on the "big bottom" first Standard Sandwich and Barber jars. The paneled candy jar was widely produced in the 1930s and is known to depression glass dealers as the Pretzel Jar. These logos are often found on peanut butter and peanut tins and as paper labels on the glass jars that were used to pack peanut-butter. The one gallon jar is often embossed in the bottom, "Lance Packing Company, Charlotte, N. Car."

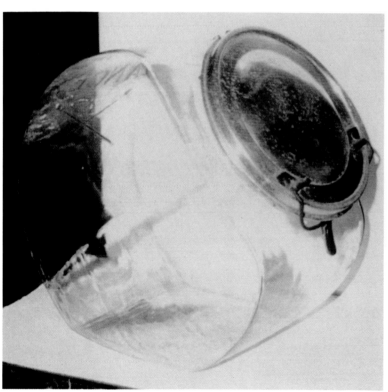

Lance Side Loader (top view), circa 1932. *Leon Helms.*

Lance™ Jars, Mid-Thirties to Mid-Forties
Lance™ Decal Jars

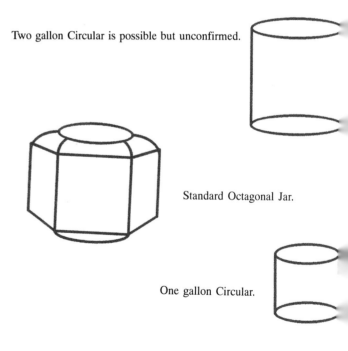

Two gallon Circular is possible but unconfirmed.

Standard Octagonal Jar.

One gallon Circular.

Lance™ octagonal, complex target logo on decal, "Lance™ Packing Company, Charlotte, N.C.,"[29] uncommon but extremely easy to reproduce — $150+, no chips and undamaged. Buyer Beware. This may also appear with a Lance™ Inc. decal but that is unconfirmed.

Lance Decal, Pretzel Jar and Octagonal Jar, circa 1938. The box is circa 1948. *Leon Helms.*

Pretzel Jar with Decal, circa 1938. *Leon Helms.*

Lance Octagonal Jar, with Lance Packing Decal, circa 1938. *Leon Helms.*

Lance Pretzel Jar Lid.

Lance™ Paneled Candy or Pretzel Jar, complex target Logo on decal, "Lance™ Packing Company, Charlotte, N.C.," uncommon but extremely easy to reproduce — $150+ no chips and undamaged. Buyer Beware. This may also appear with a Lance™ Inc. decal but that is unconfirmed. Jar is often seen unmarked for about $40.

Lance™ circular one gallon, embossed in bottom, Lance™ Packing Company, Charlotte, N. Car., complex target Logo on decal, "Lance™ Packing Company, Charlotte, N.C.," uncommon but extremely easy to reproduce — $150+ no chips and undamaged. Buyer Beware. This may also appear with a Lance™ Inc. decal but that is unconfirmed. The jar without the decal is more commonly seen.

Lance One Gallon Decal, embossed in bottom, delicate finial lid, 1938. The decal is missing from the jar. Also shown is a Lance Honor Box and Lance Packing Company Shelf Brace. Note the "four packs" inside the jar. *Leon Helms.*

Lance™ circular one gallon, complex target logo on decal, "Lance™ Packing Company, Charlotte, N.C.," uncommon but extremely easy to reproduce — $150+ no chips and undamaged. Buyer Beware. This may also appear with a Lance™ Inc. decal but that is unconfirmed.

Lance™ Packing Company Products Logo

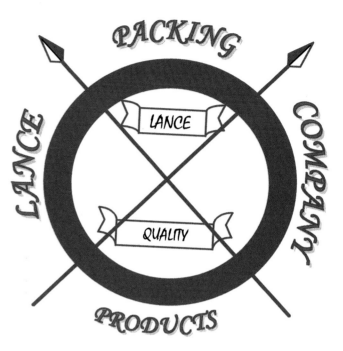

Bottom of the Lance Circular Jar, Lance Packing Co., Charlotte, N. Car. *Leon Helms.*

In the case of the Standard Lance Sandwich and Standard Barber jar, this logo was presented on the sides that were commonly left blank in later editions. It usually appears with the common crossed lances logo. However, it can be found as the only logo on these jars or with the decal target or seal logo. These jars usually have the aluminum lid with fan finial. It appears alone on four sides of the Standard Octagonal Jar. The chronology of appearance for these styles and lid types is commonly debated.

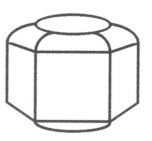

Upright view of the Lance Circular Jar showing the delicate finial lid. This jar is thought to have been a decal jar, circa 1938. *Leon Helms.*

Lance Barber, Peanut or Candy Jar.

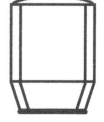

Lance Standard or Regular Jar.

Standard Octagonal Jar.

Lance™ octagonal, complex logo in blue, "Lance™ Packing Company Products," with Lance™ and Quality inside circular logo with crossed blue lances — $150+ no chips and undamaged, price determined by market.

Lance Big Bottom Jar, Barber and Sandwich, Aluminum Lids, 1938-1939. This jar is found with many lids: Over the Lip, Lance Glass Lid, late 1930s; standard "Flying A", Lance lid, late 1940s; a variation on the marking of the Standard "Flying A", Glass Lid, 1938 to 1953; Lance Tin Lid with Blue Finial, late 1930s to late 1940s; and standard Tin Replacement Lid used from the late 1930s until the mid-1960s with a standard finial; or the aluminum lid could be correct. The preferred lid is the aluminum lid with the Lance finial. Note the counter displays for Lance jars. Both of these metal counter displays date from the 1940s and 1950s. These jars never have Lance embossed in the bottom. *Leon Helms.*

Lance Octagonal Jar with a large Lance Packing Product logo, 1937. *Leon Helms.*

Octagon Lid for all Standard Octagonal Jars prior to 1940.

Lance Big Bottom Jar on the left without Lance on the bottom, Lance standard on the right.

Lance™ Packing Company Products Logo "Big Bottom" Lance™ Standard and Barber Jars

Lance™ standard Sandwich, marked Lance™ in red with crossed lances in blue, Cross E in Lance™ logo, Lance™ not embossed in bottom, this jar is slightly different in shape, early over the outside rim lid or blue composite finial on tin or aluminum lid marked Lance™ — $125 in excellent condition.

LANCE

This *Lance* logo appeared shortly before World War II. It has been observed in a very poor photograph of a circular jar that may be a two gallon standard. This jar was limited in use. This is the jar after which *Lance* patterned the 50th Anniversary Jar. The standard *Lance* jars that were developed prior to World War II went through several minor changes in logo and at least one major variation in size and mold. These variations resulted in the "big bottom," standard sandwich jars, the jars that do not have *Lance* embossed in the bottom.

Lance Big Bottom Jar Standard Sandwich, no Lance on the bottom of the jar, late 1930s. Over the Lip, Lance Glass Lid, late 1930s; standard "Flying A", Lance lid, late 1940s; a variation on the marking of the Standard "Flying A", Glass Lid, 1938 to 1953; Lance Tin Lid with Blue Finial, late 1930s to late 1940s; and standard Tin Replacement Lid used from the late 1930s until the mid-1960s with a standard finial would be considered correct. The preferred lids are the over the lip or the aluminum with Lance finial.

 Lance Barber, Peanut or Candy Jar.

Lance™ standard Sandwich, with small "Lance™ Packing Company Products" logo on the front and rear and no marking on side or decal on sides, correct lid is aluminum unpainted with blue composite finial marked Lance™[31]— $175, price determined by market and condition.

Lance™ standard Barber, marked Lance™ in red with crossed arrows, "Lance™ Packing Company Products" logo on off-side, correct lid is aluminum unpainted with blue composite finial marked Lance™[32] — $170, price determined by market and condition. (See photo 97 for the aluminum lid.)

Lance™ standard Barber, marked Lance™ in red with crossed lances in blue, Cross E in Lance™ logo, Lance™ not embossed in bottom, early over the outside rim lid, or blue composite finial marked Lance™ on tin or aluminum lid — $125 in excellent condition.

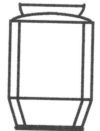 Lance Standard, Regular, or Sandwich Jar.

 Standard Circular One or Two Gallon.

Lance™ standard Sandwich, marked Lance™ in red with crossed arrows, "Lance™ Packing Company Products" logo on off-side, correct lid is aluminum unpainted with blue composite finial marked Lance™[30] — $175, price determined by market and condition. Appears with both the small and large "Lance™ Packing Company Products" logos.

Lance Barber Jar, no Lance in bottom of the jar. Over the Lip, Lance Glass Lid, late 1930s; standard "Flying A", Lance lid, late 1940s; a variation on the marking of the Standard "Flying A", Glass Lid, 1938 to 1953; Lance Tin Lid with Blue Finial, late 1930s to late 1940s; and standard Tin Replacement Lid used from the late 1930s until the mid-1960s with a standard finial would be considered correct The preferred lids for this jar are the over the lip and the aluminum with Lance finial. *Ann S. Yarborough.*

Lance™ Circular with crossed lances

Lance™ circular one gallon, marked Lance™ in red over crossed blue lances, on both sides. This is the jar the anniversary jar was patterned after — $100, price determined by market.

Lance™ Standard Jars
Late-1930s to 1953
Dates overlap in both directions

Lance™ standard Cracker, marked Lance™ in red with crossed lances, Cross E in logo, Lance™ embossed in bottom — $40-60.

Lance™ Standard Cracker, marked Lance™ in red with crossed lances, Block E in logo, Lance™ embossed in bottom — $40-$60.

Lance Standard Sandwich, Lance in bottom, Cross E. All lids listed in the previous captions would be considered correct for this jar but the most commonly encountered are the standard "Flying A" Lance lid from the late 1940s and the standard Tin Replacement Lid used from the late 1930s until the mid-1960s with a standard finial.

Lance Standard Sandwich, Block E. All lids listed in the previous captions would be considered correct for this jar but the most commonly encountered are the standard "Flying A" Lance lid from the late 1940s and the standard Tin Replacement Lid used from the late 1930s until the mid-1960s with a standard finial.

Lance™ Standard Barber, marked Lance™ in red with crossed lances, Block E in logo, Lance™ embossed in bottom — $50-$70.

Lance™ Standard Barber, marked Lance™ in red with crossed lances, Cross E in logo, Lance™ embossed in bottom — $50-$70.

Lance Barber Jar, Lance in bottom, Cross E. All lids listed in the previous captions would be considered correct for this jar but the most commonly encountered are the standard "Flying A" Lance lid from the late 1940s and the standard Tin Replacement Lid used from the late 1930s until the mid-1960s with a standard finial. *Ann S. Yarborough.*

Lance Standard Barber, Block E. All lids listed in the previous captions would be considered correct for this jar but the most commonly encountered are the standard "Flying A" Lance lid from the late 1940s and the standard Tin Replacement Lid used from the late 1930s until the mid-1960s with a standard finial. *Ann S. Yarborough.*

Lance Barber Jars Cross Arrows logos showing all three styles. *Ann S. Yarborough.*

This logo was adopted in the early 1950s. It first came into being after World War II, as a pennant on a knight's lance. As it appears on the four jars that *Lance* used from it inception until the end of *Lance's* use of jars, the block letters *L, N,* and *E* are in orange with *A* and *C* in blue. *Lance* moved to the new space saver jars in the late 1960s with the birth of the six-pack of crackers. On the jar, the pennant is tattered and " *From the house of"* is in blue print.

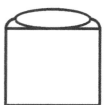

Lance Space-Saver Peanut or Candy Jar.

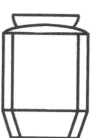

Lance Barber, Peanut, or Candy Jar.

Lance Barber Jars, all four styles. *Ann S. Yarborough.*

Lance Standard, Regular or Sandwich Jar.

Lance™ glass lids with different or large letters demand a premium, as do those that fit over the outside rim of the jar. All other standard flying A lids are common. Common tin lids never demand a premium except those with fan finials.

Lance Space-Saver Regular or Sandwich.

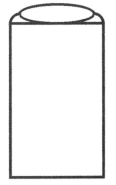

Lance™ Jars
1953 - 1967
Dates Overlap in Both Directions

Lance™ Standard Cracker, orange and blue letters, Lance™ in blue pennant on two sides, embossed Lance™ in pennant logo lid — $35-$60.

Lance Pennant Sandwich, early 1950s. Correct lids would be the standard tin replacement lid used from the late 1930s until the mid-1960s with a standard finial and the Lance Pennant lid. Others will be encountered.

Lance Pennant Lid.

Standard tin replacement lid used from late 1930s until the mid-1960s with a standard finial.

Lance™ standard Barber, orange and blue letters Lance™ in blue pennant on two sides, embossed Lance™ in pennant logo lid (barber) — $40-$65.

Replacement lids of all types were used.

Lance Pennant Barber, early 1950s. The correct lids would be the standard tin replacement lid used from the late 1930s until the mid-1960s with a standard finial and the Lance Pennant lid. Others will be encountered. *Ann S. Yarborough.*

Lance Pennant Lid.

The End of Production for Lance™ Jars 1967-1978

Lance™ standard Cracker, orange and blue letters, Lance™ in blue pennant logo on two sides, curved corners, not octagonal, 13" tall, larger mouth, tin lid. There are two distinct variations of this jar. The newer pattern appears to have a wavy pattern in the glass about 3" from the bottom, the older pattern is clear glass[33] — $45-$65.

Lance™ standard Barber, orange and blue letters, Lance™ in blue pennant on two sides, curved corners, not octagonal, 7" tall, larger mouth size, tin lids only — $50-$70. These jars are very popular with those who use jars as canister sets. The price is occasionally inflated due to this market.

Both jars have an odd mouth size and take the large tin lid.

Lance Space Saver Barber. The correct lid is the Lance Space Saver Lid.

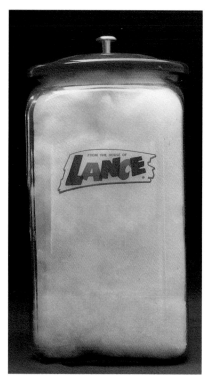

Lance Space Saver (older style with a clear panel). The correct lid is the Lance Space Saver Lid.

Lance Space Saver (newer style with a wavy panel). The correct lid is the Lance Space Saver Lid.

Lance Space Saver Lid.

Seventy-fifth Anniversary Jar

To commemorate the seventy-fifth anniversary of production, Lance™ issued jars for presentation to employees.[34] The jar depicted was presented to a Lance™ route salesman in Asheville, North Carolina. It is reported that other styles of jars were made and presented, including one that duplicates the first Lance™ Candy jar, but Lance™ cannot confirm this.[35] This jar is the Anchor-Hocking standard two gallon, large mouth , red letters, Lance™, above crossed blue lances, obverse, large 75th in blue with a red banner and white letters, "Our 75th Anniversary," white border, red letters in white box, 1913 - l988. Standard Anchor-Hocking Lid. Price determined by market. Be aware that a number of these jars were rejected during the logo application process and will not contain the date or will be damaged badly on the date panel. These jars were never given or accepted by the Lance™ Company.

Lance 75th
Anniversary Jar,
front view.

that fit over the outside rim of the jar. A steel lid with the blue composite finial also appeared, as did a variation in glass with distinct lettering. Dating the appearance of these lids is a matter of common debate.

In 1953, Lance™ pennant lids were all standardized, and a steel lid with a chrome finial was also widely used. Occasionally chrome finials from Lance™ lazy-susans were removed and placed on jars and a peanut-shaped or oval finial is also found on standard steel lids. These are associated with the earlier Barber Jars. The Space-Saver Jar had a large mouth and one lid in tin stamped Lance™ on the inside. This is the only lid that will correctly fit those jars.

Lance Apothecary Lid. *Leon Helms.*

Lance 75th
Anniversary Jar,
rear view.

Lance™ Lids

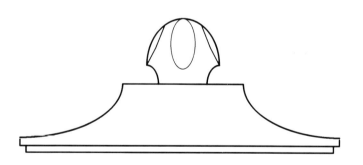

Glass lids before 1940 vary according to the jar. The slender apothecary had a typical apothecary lid. The ginger, acorn, or first sandwich used a standard lid. The one-gallon circular jars probably all used the delicate finial lid that resembles a scaled down version of the octagonal jar lid. The side-loaders and basketball or ball jars all had tin lids of different configurations. The pretzel or paneled candy had a distinct lid associated with that particular piece of clear depression glass. The octagonal sandwich jars had the standard octagonal, tear drop finial lid.

When Lance™ standardized the cracker and barber jars in the late 1930s, an aluminum lid with a blue Lance™ composite finial was used. [36] This was followed or preceded by a glass lid

The first *Lance* Sandwich Jar is the second jar which *Lance* produced. It is shaped like a ginger jar and is occasionally referred to as *The Ginger Jar*. The style was very popular and is frequently seen in an unmarked version. The glass company that produced this jar also produced marked versions of the same jar and lid for the *Squirrel Nut Company* of Cambridge, Massachusetts. The correct lid for each of these jars is similar to the lid depicted above. The *Lance* Sandwich Jar is embossed *"Lance Packing Company, Charlotte, N.C."* This jar was probably produced by the glass company that produced the first *Lance* jar, a candy jar with a fitted ground lid. The candy jar is a thin apothecary and it is believed to have been produced for a longer period of time than the Sandwich Jar.

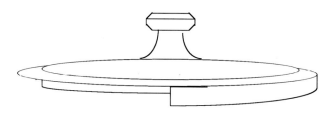

Lance Standard Glass lids come in several styles. The earliest lids fit over the outside of the lip of the jar (right side of drawing). The first adaptation was to add a seating ring and drop the rim (left side of drawing) probably in the 1940s. The *Lance* pennant was adopted in the early 1950s and the logo on the lid was changed to reflect this. *Lance* glass lids also featured two distinct styles of lettering in the Flying A lids.

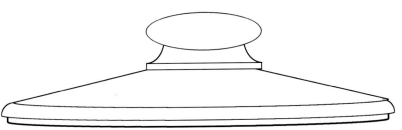

The *Lance* standard Octagon was adopted in the late 1930s or early 1940s and although stylized, was used until production of jars ceased. However, *Lance* used the octagonal shape much earlier. Beginning early in the 1920s, a number of logos were used on an octagon jar. The earliest of these jars is embossed *"Lance Packing Company"* over crossed lances in a circle over *Charlotte, N.C.* Next in chronology was the *"Insist on Lance's"* style painted logo. Finally, *Lance* produced the octagonal jars with the *Lance* Decal and the *"Lance Packing Company Products"* logo. All of the these jars carried a lid with a teardrop finial similar to the one depicted above. The lid used on the standard one-gallon circular jar appears to be a delicate scaled down version of this lid.

Over the lip, Lance glass lid, late 1930s.

Standard "Flying A", Lance lid, late 1940s.

Octagon Lid for all Standard Octagonal Jars prior to 1940.

Variation of the marking in the standard "Flying A", Glass Lid, 1938 to 1953.

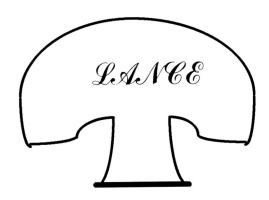

The *Lance* fan finial has *Lance* in white on a blue plastic composite fan or peanut-shaped finial. This finial is seen on both the aluminum and the steel lids. A large aluminum Lance finial is also seen bearing the later pennant logo. This large pennant logo finial is associated with the *Lance* Lazy-Susan rather than the jars. This illustrated finial was used on both jars and the Lazy-Susan.

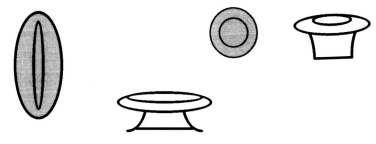

The oblong or oval finial is often found on the common red steel lid. Some observers believe it is peanut-shaped and should be displayed on the Barber or Peanut Jar. This is the common circular finial that is often seen on the larger Cracker or Sandwich Jar.

The common red steel lid is associated with both the Barber and Sandwich Jars of *Lance*. It was the standard replacement for glass lids in the years following the adaptation of a *Lance* Standard. It was replaced by the large red steel lid that is used with the later jars. By far, the most common *Lance* lid, it is stamped *Lance* on the underside.

Lance Tin Lid with Blue Finial, late 1930s to late 1940s.

Standard Tin Replacement Lid used from late 1940s until the mid-1960s with a standard finial.

Lance Pennant Lid.

Lance Pennant Lid.

The last *Lance* lid is also a red steel lid and is larger than the standard size. It vaguely resembles this depiction and is marked *Lance* inside the lid.

Lance logo on an early display rack, circa 1938. *Leon Helms.*

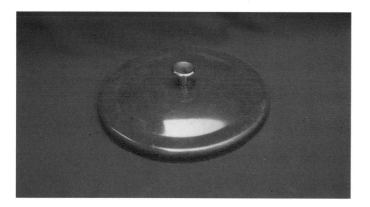

Lance Space Saver Lid.

A word about *Lance* and its lettering, *the flying A* refers to the tail at the top of the *A* like the letter *A* that is shown on the left. The *flying A* is found on many Lance jars but is associated with Lance's first standard jars that were introduced around 1940. The earliest of the *flying A* jars also had the crossed *E* like the *E* on the far right. The center bar crosses and extends to the left of the upright bar on the letter *E* in this style. These early Lance standard jars are not uniform and the most unusual does not carry *Lance* embossed in the bottom of the jar. The larger or Sandwich Jar in this style has a distinct shape that is slightly different. At some point in the production of these early standard jars, The *"Lance Packing Company Products"* logo was placed on what later became the blank side of both the Sandwich and Barber jars. These two standards, the larger Cookie or Sandwich and the smaller Barber, Peanut, or Candy would be associated with the Lance Company until jar production ceased.

Lance Display Rack, made in Charlotte, circa 1938. *Leon Helms.*

Lance Five Pound Peanut Tin, paper label, World War II.

Lance Potato Chip Can, late 1940s, paper label, note the script logo. *Leon Helms.*

Lance Potato Chip Can (1946) and Box (late 1930s or early 1940s). *Leon Helms,*

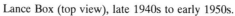

Lance Box, late 1940s, end view showing the Target or Seal Logo.

Lance Box (top view), late 1940s to early 1950s.

Lance Box, late 1940s, side showing the Charlotte plant.

Lance Peanut Butter Jar, 1930s. *Leon Helms.*

Lance Box, circa 1965.

Lance Club Cracker Box, circa 1938. *Leon Helms.*

Lance Peanut Butter Jar, circa 1938. *Leon Helms.*

Lance Club Cracker Box, circa 1938. *Leon Helms.*

68

Lance Peanut Butter Jar, circa 1950. *Leon Helms.*

Lance Four Jar Wire Rack Sign, circa 1955. *Leon Helms.*

Lance Door Push Sign, 1940s. *Leon Helms.*

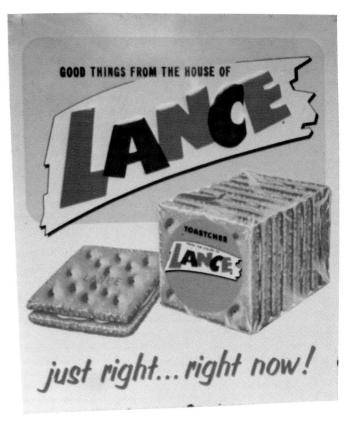

Lance Four Jar Wire Rack Sign, circa 1964. *Leon Helms.*

Lance Four Jar Wire Rack Sign, circa 1970. *Leon Helms.*

Lance Six Jar Wire Rack Sign, circa 1955. *Leon Helms.*

Lance Six Jar Wire Rack Sign, circa 1970. *Leon Helms.*

Lance Porcelain Tray, probably used at food shows. *Leon Helms.*

Special thanks to Leon Helms, a long time Lance™ employee and collector, who has carefully collected and recorded the history of Lance™. Without his help this project would certainly not be what it is. Leon remains the authority on Lance™ and its history. If other jars exist, and they probably do, Leon will be the one to confirm or deny them.

My thanks to Hall Lance™ for sharing his collection, knowledge and friendship with me.

Thanks also goes to Lawrence Knighton, who rented me my first apartment, built my home, and taught me about the love of collecting old jars and cans.

B.C. McWhite and his family remain close friends and his memories have provided a special look at Lance™, Goodest Foods, and this industry that is very nearly lost.

Lance receipt, circa 1927. *Leon Helms.*

QUEEN CHARLOTTE BRAND
FINEST QUALITY
PEANUT BUTTER

TRADE MARK REGISTERED

Enlargement of the Lance logo on the receipt. Note Queen Charlotte Brand Peanut Butter. *Leon Helms.*

Lance receipt, mid-1930s. Obverse shows Logos and Peanut Butter Jar. *Leon Helms.*

Lance receipts, circa 1934. *Leon Helms.*

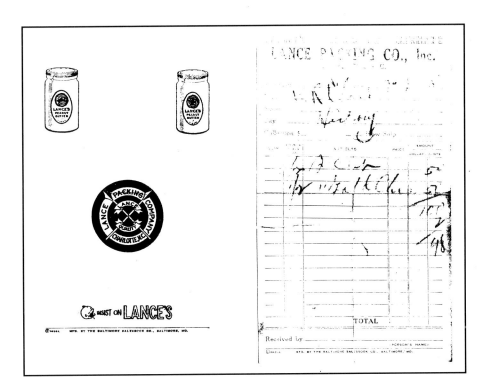

MANUFACTURERS OF PEANUT FOOD PRODUCTS
PLANTS - CHARLOTTE, N. C., GREENVILLE, TEXAS

Lance logos, mid-1930s and at bottom 4 pack logo from the 1950s. *Leon Helms.*

Lance receipt, circa 1938, Richmond, Virginia. *Leon Helms.*

Lance receipt, circa 1939. Note the use of Lance Inc. *Leon Helms.*

Lance receipt, circa 1954. Note the four pack. *Leon Helms.*

QUEEN CHARLOTTE BRAND
FINEST QUALITY
PEANUT BUTTER

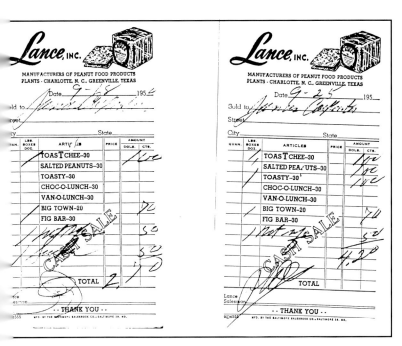

TRADE MARK REGISTERED

Lance logo, circa mid-1920s. *Leon Helms.*

Lance receipt, circa mid-1950s. Note the script L in the logo and four pack. *Leon Helms.*

STORE OR DISPLAY JARS:

The first three documented Lance™ jars are all embossed and were introduced prior to 1920 or early in the 1920s. Do other jars exist? Most probably they do, but Leon Helms will remain the authority.

The earliest was the slender Apothecary Jar or Candy Jar. It is embossed Lance™ Packing Company, Charlotte, N.C. and has a ground lid like a traditional apothecary. (Jar Number One — this listing is a quick reference and the jar numbers are arbitrary and strictly for the reader's convenience.)

The Sandwich Jar is often called the Ginger Jar because of its shape and is also embossed Lance™ Packing Company, Charlotte, N.C. (Jar Number Two)

The Octagonal Sandwich was also introduced about this time and was embossed Lance™ Packing Company, Charlotte, N.C. with a circle and crossed lances also embossed in the glass. (Jar Number Three)

The next series of jars introduced by Lance™ carry a blue or red fired-on, painted logo that says, "Insist on Lance's™" over crossed blue lances.

The Ball or Basketball Jar of the Twenties is often seen with the red logo and is reported with a blue logo. This jar was made in two sizes, a one gallon and a smaller version. (Jar Number Five and Six as the blue logo is unconfirmed.)

The Octagonal Sandwich Jar is found usually marked in blue on four of the eight sides with this logo. (Jar Number Seven)

The one gallon circular jar is also commonly found marked on two sides with this logo. This jar would carry the delicate finial lid. (Jar Number Eight)

A side-loading jar marked with this logo is also reported. It has a rather complex closure system on at least one example. (Jar Number Nine)

In the thirties a decal jar was issued in the octagonal shape and also a common Pretzel Jar in clear glass was used as a candy jar with the decal logo. Both of these jars are difficult to obtain with the original decal. This jar is also found in the one and two gallon circular styles with Lance™ Packing Company, Charlotte, N.Car. embossed in the bottom of the one gallon jar (Jars Number Ten, Eleven, Twelve, and Thirteen)

The last of the true octagonal jars bears the Lance™ Packing Company logo in blue on four of the eight sides. (Jar Number Fourteen)

A circular two-gallon jar is also listed by the Lance™ Company bearing the red Lance™ and crossed lances in blue on both sides. (Jar Number Fifteen)

Around 1940, Lance™ standardized its jars with a modified octagonal jar. This jar is seen in a number of variations including the following: flying A jars appear in both the Barber and Sandwich sizes. Jars in both sizes with the Lance™ Packing Company complex logo on what later became the blank sides are known. Jars with just the Lance™ Packing Company Products logo and jars with both the Lance™ Packing Company logos and jars with both the Lance™ Packing Company logos and the decal or target logo. The earliest examples have a crossed E and lack the word Lance™ embossed in the bottom. Both the Barber and regular jars are also found with Lance™ embossed in the bottom and the crossed E and both are found without the crossed E. At least four distinct variations and eight versions of both the regular and Barber jars exist. Variations in the size of the Lance™ Packing Company logo account for other examples. (Jars Number Sixteen through Twenty-three, at least)

In the early Fifties the pennant logo was introduced on both the Sandwich and Barber jars. In the Sixties, the tall space-saving jar with two distinct variations and its barber-sized companion were the last of the Lance™ jars. (Jars Number Twenty-four through Twenty-eight)

The anniversary jar (Jar Number Twenty-nine).

OTHER LANCE PRODUCTION ITEMS OF INTEREST TO THE COLLECTOR INCLUDE:

LABELING FOR PACKAGING:

Four pack pull tabs.
Paper labels.

BULK PEANUT AND CRACKER TINS:

Five and ten lb., Lance™ painted tins in blue from the thirties.

Five pound tins for peanuts with paper labels from the forties.

Five and ten pound cracker tins from both eras.
Lance™ potato chip tin with paper labels.

Lance Club Cracker Box, circa 1938. *Leon Helms.*

Lance Club Cracker Box, circa 1938. *Leon Helms.*

PEANUT BUTTER ITEMS:

Glass jars with paper labels for peanut butter.

Peanut butter tins with paper labels from the thirties and forties.

Peanut butter pails in small sizes from the twenties, thirties and forties.

Lance Peanut Butter Pail (side view). *Photo Leon Helms. Hall Lance Collection.*

Lance Five Pound Salted Peanut Tin, printed can. *Leon Helms.*

PAPER ITEMS:

Candy, peanut and cracker boxes from all eras.
Stamped shirt boxes from the teens.
Printed candy boxes from the twenties.
Printed cracker and candy boxes from the forties.

TIN OR OTHER SIGNS:

Tin screen door push sign that depicts a pretty girl enjoying Lance™ Peanuts.

The six signs associated with the racks of the forties, fifties, and sixties.

Lance Endnotes

[1] *The History of Lance*™, undated publication, Lance™ Inc.
[2] Interview Leon Helms, 1994.
[3] Lance™ History.
[4] Ibid.
[5] Helms interview.
[6] Lance™ publication, undated circular, Lance™ Inc.
[7] *Lance™ Candy*, undated publication, Lance™ Inc.
[8] *History of Lance*™ *Jars,* undated handbill, Lance™ Inc.
[9] Ibid.
[10] Helms interview.
[11] Ibid.
[12] Ibid.
[13] *Lance™ Jars.*
[14] *Lance™ History.*
[15] B.C. McWhite interviews.
[16] *Lance™ History.*
[17] Interview with Leon Helms.
[18] Ibid.
[19] Ibid.
[20] *Lance™ History.*
[21] Ibid.
[22] Letter, Tom Ingram, Lance™ Inc.
[23] *Lance™ History.*
[24] Hal Lance, interview; Helms interview.
[25] *Lance™ History.*
[26] Ingram letter.
[27] *Lance™ History.*
[28] Ingram letter.
[29] Helms interview.
[30] Ibid.
[31] Ibid.
[32] Ibid.
[33] Ibid.
[34] Ibid, Lance™ interview.
[35] Ingram letter.
[36] Helms interview.

Leaf Confectionery

Leaf Confectionery was a division of Beatrice Foods. In December of 1983, Huhtamaki Oy, a Finnish conglomerate bought the Leaf Division. Among the well-known candies controlled by Leaf were the old Heath Brothers, Hollywood Brands, Jolly Rancher, Warner-Lambert, and Switzer Candies as well as the Leaf brand.

The old Heath Bar was produced by the Heath Brothers in Robinson, Illinois. The candy first entered production in 1914. Heath was acquired by Leaf in 1989. Switzer Licorice dates from 1916 and was acquired by Leaf during the merger with Beatrice Confectionery Division.

Overland Candy produced malted milk balls that in 1949 were dubbed Whoppers, but the malted milk confection had long been in production before that name was adopted. Overland was acquired by Leaf in 1947. Milk Duds, another Leaf product, was originally produced by F. Hoffman and Co. of Chicago in 1926. Leaf also controlled Good'n Plenty which was introduced in 1883 by Quaker City Confectionery.

One of the best known lines of the Leaf Company was Hollywood Brands. In the 1960s, Hollywood was extremely large in volume of production. Hollywood began as the brainchild of Frank Martoccio of the Martoccio Macaroni Company. He began candy production in 1933. By 1936, candy production out-weighed macaroni sales and the macaroni company was divested. In 1967, Hollywood was sold to Consolidated Foods Inc. and in 1988, Leaf acquired Hollywood Brands. Hollywood controlled candies that predate the formation of their company including Zagnut (1916), Polar (1924), and Payday (1934). The Milkshake bar and the Zero bar were both developed in 1933 and were the original Hollywood products. Leaf also controlled Bill Harmsen's Jolly Rancher Candy Company founded in 1949 in Golden, Colorado. This company included the Stix line of candies.

Leaf Candies production lines:

Rainblo Gum	1940
Quaker City Confectionery	
Good 'n Plenty	1883
Heath Brothers	
(Robinson, IL.)	
Heath Bars	1914
Switzer Licorice	1916
F.A. Martoccio Co.	1933
Hollywood Brands	1936
Zagnut	1916
Polar	1924
Pay Day	1932
Milkshake	1933
Zero	1933
Rancher (Golden, Co.)	1949
Overand Candy Company	
Whoppers named in	1949
F. Hoffman and Company	
(Chicago, IL.)	
Milk Duds	1926

So Big Box, Quaker City Confectionery, circa World War II.

Lummis Salted Nuts

LUMMIS
Salted
Peanuts

Lummis logo as it appears on the one gallon jar.

A one-gallon standard Anchor-Hocking marked Lummis Salted Nuts. No other information is available on the Lummis line. Jar would cost $30-$45.

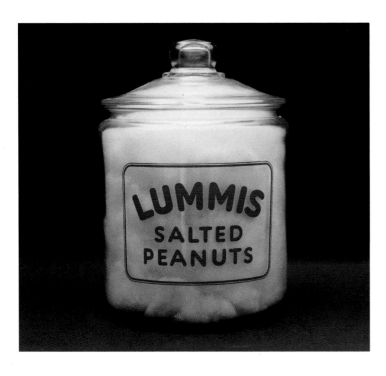

Lummis Salted Nuts, One Gallon, circa 1955.

Mars/M & M
Tacoma, Washington, Chicago, Illinois
1911

Franklin C. Mars began making candy in his home in 1911. From that humble beginning, the candy giant of today grew. Moving to Minneapolis, Minnesota, in the early twenties, he developed his milk chocolate confections and began production of the Milky Way Bar shortly after the move.

The central production facility was moved to Chicago in 1929 and production continues at that site. Following a split with his father, Forrest Mars Sr. went to England and started a confectionery business of his own. He established the first canned pet food industry in England and carried the Mars business flag around the world.

Forrest Mars Sr. returned to the United States and established M&M Limited in Newark, New Jersey, in 1940. He began production of Plain M&M's at that site. It was emphasized that the new candy was a neat, convenient treat that could be eaten in almost any climate. The company continued production during World War II for the United States military. His development of parboiled rice for the US military led to the Uncle Ben's line.

In 1954, the slogan, "The milk chocolate melts in your mouth-not in your hand," was developed to stress product convenience. In 1967, all Mars candies consolidated to become M&M/Mars, the company that we know today.

Candy Bar	Date of Development
Milky Way	1923
Snickers	1930
3 Musketeers	1932
Mars Almond Bar	1936
Dove Bar	1939
M&M's plain	1940
M&M's peanut	1954
Snickers Munch Bar	1970
Skittles	1974
Combos Snacks	1981
Twix	1982
M&M's almonds	1984*
M&M's mint chocolate	1988
Dove Chocolate (Marketed Nationally)	1992
Milky Way lite	1994

*Brought back to the line in 1984

Mars/M&M's
Dove Candies

Dove Candies began as a small candy shop on the south side of Chicago. It was founded by Leo Stephanos, a Greek emigrant, in 1939. In 1956 he introduced the Dove Bar. It was sold by street carts until being introduced to supermarkets.

In 1986 Dove International became a division of Mars Candies. In 1993 Dove International became a part of M&M/Mars.

Ethel M. Chocolates, Inc.

This company was established in Las Vegas, Nevada in 1978 to produce a premium boxed chocolate for the Mars line. Today it manufactures over sixty different premium chocolate brands.

Colors of M&M's

The mystery of the colors of M&M's coating is addressed in the wonderful publication M&M's * Mars colors. It is available by request from Mars Incorporated. Blue was added in September 1995. Blue replaced tan in the plain and orange in the peanut butter and almond mix.

For Valentine's Day reds, pinks, and white are added to the candy mix. At Easter pastel shades of yellow, blue, green, pink and purple are added. At Christmas the mix is 50% red and 50% green.

Mars claims no special powers can be attributed to eating green M&M's but we all know better. All trademarks, logos, and characters are the sole property of Mars Incorporated.

Maryland Biscuit Company

Maryland Biscuit was an old southern company that is thought to have been based in Baltimore, Maryland. It operated heavily in North Carolina, East Tennessee, and South Carolina. Absorbed by Murray, its history is for the moment lost. Any information about the company would be appreciated.

Maryland Biscuit Company Store Tin — $55-$75.

This Maryland Biscuit Tin has no glass and three paper labels as shown. The bottom label shows a loaf of Maryland Biscuit Bread and tells the buyer to ask for it here. The blue seal is printed Maryland Biscuit Co. This tin has Maryland Biscuit Co. embossed at the edge of the covering lip. The labels are very faded on this example, but the dominant colors were red and yellow or red and white. The label is shown with white.

Maryland Biscuit Large Tin, 1900-1930.

Maryland Standard Tins Paper Label — $15-$35.

This small Maryland Biscuit tin is typical. The paper label is poor quality and has aged brown. The letters were maroon with a white or yellow highlight. The blue border with white inserts was delicate in design.

Maryland Biscuit Small Tin, 1900-1930.

Maryland Tin, 1935-1955.

Maryland Box Front, 1935-1955.

Maryland Box fronts, nickel plated — $15-$25, with Maryland cardboard box a slight premium would be added to the price.

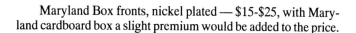

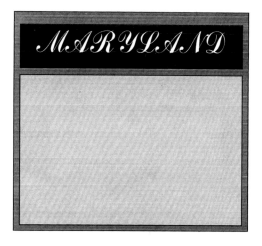

Maryland Biscuit Company was a large firm, probably from Maryland. Box fronts are found across the South and are generally of a lesser quality than Nabisco. This frame is nickel-plated with Maryland embossed on a textured background. This practice eliminated the possibility of replacing the name if the competition took control of your sales.

Maryland Box Front, 1935-1955.

This Maryland box front has a name plate that attaches to the box front and may be detached or replaced. The colors are brown gold for the frame with a maroon background and gold letters for the plate. These fronts appear to be more common than the silver frame. Neither would be considered uncommon in the South.

Mitchum and Tucker Sandwiches
Charlotte, N.C.
1937-

One gallon standard, red letters, "M & T Toasted Peanuts," in red script letters — $25-$40.

Mitchum and Tucker is a Charlotte-based company and is still in production as Mitchum Inc. The company was founded by H.C. Mitchum and C.B. Tucker in 1937 as the Mitchum and Tucker Company. Mr. Mitchum was a grocer who went in the candy business on a doctor's advice. He started with candy and expanded into peanut butter and cheese crackers in the late forties. Mr. H.C. Mitchum Jr. joined the firm in the late fifties. In 1961, Mitchum Sr. bought Mr. Tucker's interest in the company.

At this time, potato chips were added to the product mix. Selling chips and crackers to grocery chains to be marketed under house labels as "Stay Fresh" became the mainstay of the product line. Mitchum also packaged under the "Morning Fresh" label as well as the Mitchum label. The senior Mitchum's stated goal was to strive for a productive living, producing a quality product and he survived in the sight of Lance™, Inc.

In 1966, the company moved from its Gordon Street location to its current home on Davidson Street. In 1966, Flowers Industries bought Mitchum and when they divested themselves of the company, M&T was purchased by John Wilson.

The jars are most often seen in North Carolina and South Carolina but they have also turned up in Tennessee and Virginia with some regularity. Mr. H.C. Mitchum Jr. has no recollection of a two gallon jar being used for distribution but two types have been located.

Mr. H.C. Mitchum Jr. of Charlotte, North Carolina, kindly provided the information contained in this article by furnishing a photocopy of an article that first appeared in "The Business Journal."

Mitchum and Tucker One Gallon, circa 1950.

Mitchum and Tucker Toasted Peanut logo as found on the one gallon jar.

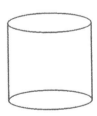

Mitchum and Tucker Sandwich logo as found on both the two gallon and side-loader.

Two gallon standard, red letters, "Mitchum & Tucker Sandwiches" — $35-$55.

Mitchum and Tucker: Two Gallon, circa 1955. *Ann S. Yarborough.*

Red letters, "Mitchum & Tucker Sandwiches," standard side-loader, lid should be metal standard neck, two distinct versions of this jar are seen — $35-$60.

Mitchum and Tucker: Side Loader, circa 1955, marked Anchor-Hocking.

Mitchum and Tucker: Side Loader, circa 1955, unmarked.

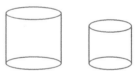

Mitchum and Tucker logo found on both the one and two gallon jars.

One gallon standard, blue circle around red "M & T," clear on red panel, Peanut Products, "Mitchum Inc., Charlotte, N.C." — $25-$40.

Mitchum and Tucker One Gallon, circa 1960.

Two gallon standard, blue circle around red "M & T," clear on red panel, Peanut Products, "Mitchum Inc., Charlotte, N.C." — $35-$60.

Mitchum and Tucker: Two Gallon, circa 1960.

Meadors' Candy
1919-1964
Greenville, South Carolina

Meadors' Sandwich Company
1946-1964

The Meadors' Candy Company began in 1919 in Greenville, South Carolina. Its early ancestor was the Meadors' Grocery located in downtown Greenville. Originally known as Meadors' Manufacturing Company and/or Blue Ridge Candy Company, two brothers, Morris and Pascal Meadors, established the company. In 1921 it was located on South Main Street near the Reedy River, next door to the Pepsi Cola Bottling Works. The address in 1923 was 467 South Main, the same location. Pascal is remembered as the salesman (a flamboyant man) and Morris, as the businessman.

Meadors' first jar was the yellow-lettered octagonal jar. It was followed by the one gallon standard with only the name Meadors in yellow letters. Although it is not established, it is thought that the standard two gallon with yellow letters also exists.

As Greenville industrialized following World War I, Meadors' Sandwich and Candy Company grew by furnishing food products to the surrounding textile mills and mill communities. During World War II, Meadors' continued to grow and built a new facility on New Buncombe Road that served as the Meadors' Sandwich Company.

In 1945, the company was known as Meadors' Manufacturing Company: candy and peanut products. The yellow-lettered side loading sandwich jar dates from this era. Meadors'

Mitchum and Tucker: One Gallon (1955), Side Loader (1955), and One Gallon (1960).

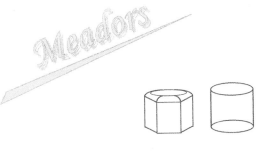

Meadors yellow logo as seen on the octagonal and one gallon jars.

Yellow letters, Meadors' Products, octagonal jar, glass teardrop lid — $75-$100

continued to refine and expand its distribution system, reaching into Georgia and North Carolina. National advertising in the fifties and sixties spoke to the size of the company as it reached across the South and the nation.

In 1964, the company was sold to United Biscuit Company that later became Keebler Cookies. Red and orange-lettered Meadors' jars date to the fifties and later.

It is believed, but not established, that the red-lettered one and two gallon jars predate the orange-lettered jars. The two gallon red-lettered jar features a distinct tin lid and finial. The grandson of one of the founders and his sons have established a new Meadors' Sandwich Company and are currently expanding with two Greenville locations, one on Poinsett Highway and a second on Augusta Road. A new process for boiling peanuts may provide this new company with a base that will allow it to grow far beyond their grandfather's dreams.

The Meadors' family report a multiple size canister set but it is unclear if this was a distribution item or a courtesy item from the glass company. The family also has an unmarked ball jar and a variety of unmarked apothecary canisters. The family believes these were all used as distribution jars. Certainly the company used many types and styles of jars with paper labels. Meadors' also used cookie boxes made from oak for the distribution of their products as well as standard racks and shelves. Meadors' oak and cypress sandwich flats are occasionally seen as are Meadors' Peanut Butter Jars (paper label).

Early Meador's containers are most often found in northern Georgia and South Carolina but Meadors' distribution was throughout the Southeast and spreading nationally when bought by United Biscuit.

My thanks to the descendants of the Meadors' family who currently operate the Meadors' Sandwich Shops in Greenville for much of this information. Also Voncie Deitz, whose mother, Ms. Jordan, was an employee of the original candy company. Meadors' (Greenville, S.C.)

The Octagon Lid for all Standard Octagonal Jars prior to 1940 is the correct lid.

Yellow letters, Meadors, one gallon standard — $35-$50.

Meadors Yellow One Gallon, 1920-1946.

Meadors Yellow Octagon (1920-1946). The Octagon Lid for all Standard Octagonal Jars prior to 1940 is the correct lid.

Meadors yellow Sandwich logo from the flip lid side-loader.

Yellow letters, "Meadors' Delicious Sandwiches 5 cents," circular from side, standard neck attachment, tin lid, had a yellow and brown insert — $35-$65.

Meadors Sandwich Side Loader, 1946-1950.

Meadors Red: Two Gallon, 1940-1950.

Meadors red logo as seen on the two gallon circular.

Meadors Two Gallon Lid with Lance Finial.

Red letters, "Meadors' Products Always Fresh," standard large cylinder red tin lid with octagonal plastic finial, but is seen with glass replacement lid — $45-$70.

Meador's red logo as seen on the one gallon circular.

Red letters, "Meadors' Products Always Fresh," standard small cylinder, glass lid — $40-$60.

Meadors Orange: Two Gallon, 1950-1960.

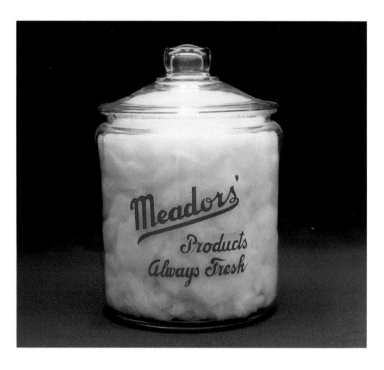

Meadors One Gallon, 1940-1950.

Orange letters "Meadors' Products Always Fresh," standard small cylinder, glass lid — $25-$50.

Meadors orange logo as found on the one and two gallon circular and the side-loader.

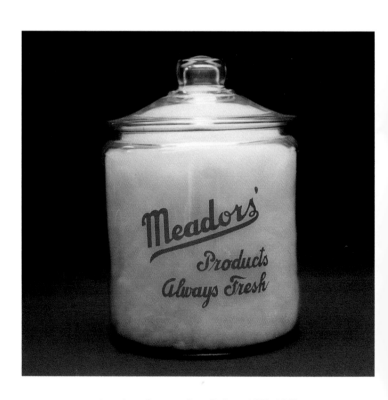

Meadors Orange: One Gallon, 1950-1960.

Orange letters "Meadors Products Always Fresh," standard large cylinder, glass lid — $35-$50.

Orange letters, "Meadors' Products Always Fresh," circular from side, standard neck attachment tin lid, originally had a cardboard or leather orange insert for lid with Meadors' logo — $25-$55.

Meadors Orange:
Side Loader, 1950-1960.

Meadors Sandwich Flat, circa 1955.

Meadors Red One and Two Gallon and Yellow Side Loader.

Meadors Sandwich Flat, circa 1955.

Meadors Orange One and Two Gallon and Side Loader.

Meadors Peanut Butter Jar, circa 1955.

Meadors lid insert for the yellow flip lid sandwich side-loader.

Meadors Canister Set, circa 1955.

Meadors Octagonal Finial lid for the two gallon red circular logo.

Meadors Jars, unmarked jars and sandwich flat, circa 1955. These jars were all used by the Meadors Company and were retained within the family.

The Meadors building appears on the far right.

Meador's Peanut Butter label and top.

Moore's Quality Snacks
Bristol, Virginia
1924-

J.W. Moore, like so many of the men who pioneered the snack food industry, was a mechanical genius and a twentieth century renaissance man. He built and designed his own equipment and help found a branch of an industry that was as familiar to the rural South during the post World War I depression as the match girl of the industrial North. In an era where men believed that sweat, industry, and creativity could not only feed a family but build a nation; these men were even then a breed apart.

In April of 1924, Mr. Moore built a potato chip fryer in his basement at the corner of Moore and Chester Streets in Bristol, Virginia. Peeling, slicing, frying, and packing chips by hand, Mr. Moore would fry at night and load his Model T up and sell by day. As demand grew, Mr. Moore added his wife to the production team. Mrs. Moore was a part of the team, and perhaps even the heart and soul of it, from the very beginning. It certainly can be said that no man of vision ever saw his dream fulfilled without the backing of a strong family.

As the home industry grew, Mr. Moore added a peanut roaster and blancher. Ever mindful that opportunity came to those who labored to find it, Mr. Moore shortly added a line of pure sugar stick candy and purchased a mill to grind peanut butter. Composition cracker sandwiches followed as did peanut butter in jars and the peanut butter candy that was preferred in the south.

Unlike chocolate, peanut butter candy maintained its flavor and, more importantly, resisted the unforgiving southern heat. A distribution system was soon organized to enhance marketing. During this period, Mr. Moore's daughter, Zella, married Tom Arnold and both entered the family business. Two sons, Jack and Joe, were born in the Great Depression and they too would follow their grandfather's vision. Unlike most businesses, the food business grew by leaps and bounds during the Great Depression.

Material and production costs were low and the New South's industry provided a natural market. By World War II, Moore's was distributing in about an eighty mile radius of Bristol. The isolation of the mountains helped to hold the large companies at bay while smaller ones fought in this small market.

World War II was a crisis for any industry depending on sugar for production and gasoline for distribution. Mr. Moore, along with Tom and Zella Arnold, struggled to keep the budding company alive. The war industry allowed the worker little time to prepare meals at home, so the snack industry was the natural benefactor. The problem was production. Mrs. Zella Arnold spoke of going to Kroger's and fighting over the sugar needed to make the candy. This was a common experience that resulted in the less determined falling by the wayside.

Moore's was apparently unable to exploit the defense industry to meet their needs. The end result was that much effort was needed to keep the company afloat during these tough years. J.W. Moore died in 1950 and management moved to Tom and Zella Arnold.

In 1956, Jack Arnold entered the business and his brother Joe joined in 1960. In 1964, it became apparent that a new facility was needed and for the first time since its founding Moore's moved, occupying the site currently used today. In May 1966, the new 23,000 square foot facility was opened. Shortly there-

after, the size of the facility was doubled and growth continued unabated through the seventies and eighties.

In 1988, fire, the bane of human existence, struck Moore's. In a catastrophic fire the entire Moore's plant and operation except for the main manufacturing section and the company offices were destroyed. Thanks to the determination of the ownership and the employees, the company was able to survive. In 1989, Moore's was sold to Borden's. Later that year long-time president and guiding light, Mrs. Zella Moore Arnold, died following a long battle with cancer. Jack and Joe continued with the company until 1992.

Today, Moore's owns over 300 company routes across the South, providing the same fine quality and freshness that are its trademarks. Its products reach satisfied customers in Virginia, Tennessee, West Virginia, Kentucky, North and South Carolina, Georgia, and Alabama.

Moore's used distribution jars in the forties and fifties. The last jars were the standard Anchor-Hocking one and two gallon units that are pictured. Moore's used at least one other logo and two earlier jars during the forties and early fifties respectively.

While shopping for jars in Bristol, I met a very kind gentleman who said he remembered "Old Man" Moore. He spoke so fondly, I asked if he could tell me about Mr. Moore. He laughed and said, "Well, back in the thirties I was a young man and wanted a job so I went to see old Mr. Moore. I went to the house and he told me to come in the kitchen and sit down which I did. There was a couple of women sitting around the table spreading peanut butter on crackers and I thought to myself, 'Old man, you are going to surely starve.' Well, I thanked him for the time and told him I appreciated the offer of a job which I had asked for but I guess I had better look around some more. The guy who took that job stayed with Mr. Moore and died a rich man and well ... look at me."

Thanks to Jim Arnold, Merchandising Manager of Moore's, for his kind assistance in providing this information. Moore's continues to thrive and grow and we wish it the best in the future. All trademarks and slogans are the sole property of Moore's Quality Snack Foods Division of Borden's Foods.

For additional information, contact Jim Arnold, Merchandising Manager, Moore's Quality Snack Foods, Inc., Box 1909, Bristol Va., 24203.

Late 1950s

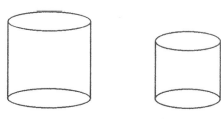

Moore's last jar logo as it appears on both the one and two gallon jars.

Red "Moore's" logo, standard large cylinder, glass lid — $35-$60.

Moore's: Two
Gallon, circa 1955.

Red "Moore's" logo, standard small cylinder, glass lid —
$25-$50.

Moore's: One
Gallon, circa 1955.

National Biscuit Company
Nabisco
1898-

Nabisco began in 1898 with the merger of the American Biscuit Company, the New York Biscuit Company, and the United States Baking Company. The American Biscuit Company had been the result of the merger of forty bakeries and the New York Biscuit Company that represented eight bakeries. National Biscuit, with a total of over one hundred bakeries, had

a virtual monopoly over the cracker and cookie market after the merger.[1]

Adolphus Green negotiated the original American Biscuit Company merger and remained as the head and guiding light of National Biscuit for over twenty years.[2] Among the original bakeries of New York Biscuit, American Biscuit, and the United States Baking Company, we find the names of John Pearson and Son Wholesale Bakers founded in 1792 in Newburyport, Massachusetts, Bent's Bakery of Milton, Massachusetts, founded in 1801 and creator of the Bent's handmade water cracker, Kennedy Biscuit Works founded in 1805 and the company that used Henry Mitchell's marvelous machine to make the fig newton, and Sommer-Richardson Baking Co. of St. Joseph, Missouri. This company manufactured premium saltines under the Red Cross label.[3] Adolphus Green's idea of standardized brand-name products was introduced when the Uneeda Biscuit brought marketing into the twentieth century and set the standards that are taken for granted today. Even the symbol of the company, the distinct double cross over an oval, became a signpost that assured uniform quality. Quality assurance with national advertising and innovative packaging became the hallmarks of National Biscuit.

Uneeda Biscuits, an ordinary soda cracker in an extraordinary package, (the "In-er-Seal" lined box) was the primer product of National Biscuit. In 1912 Lorna Doone and Oreo were created.[4] Early bulk tins for both products are highly desirable collectibles.

In 1917 Nabisco reached a watershed. Adolphus Green died and was replaced by Roy E. Tomlinson. Tomlinson continued to exploit the images created by Green. He linked Nabisco with Uncle Sam and the growing nation.[5] National Biscuit produced rations for the government and, like the entire country, was embroiled in the First World War.

The glass and tin brass front container acts as the backdrop for one of the most common of Nabisco ads. This ad features both Uncle Sam and Nabisco products. However unchanging Nabisco advertising might have remained, Tomlinson's management style was much more in tune with the new century and National Biscuit was the beneficiary.[6] Judge Moore, another of the early movers of the company, continued to add stability while Tomlinson provided a fresh new energy.

In the 1920s, National Biscuit moved into the Canadian market and acquired more diverse holdings including the Shredded Wheat Company. The 1923 product line of National Biscuit included Alphabets and Log Cabin Brownies, two items whose packaging is very collectable in today's market. In 1925, York Pretzel of York, Pennsylvania, joined the Nabisco family. In 1931, the F.W. Bennett Biscuit Company of New York was bought by Nabisco. The Bennett Company brought a full line of crackers but it was the dog treat, Milk Bone, that was to survive in the Nabisco line. The 1928 addition of the 5 cent "Nab" pack was just in time to feed the hungry during the great depression. Ritz Cracker joined the Nabisco line in 1934. The Mickey Mouse Cracker was a highlight product of the late thirties.[7]

In 1941, the letters N.B.C. were officially traded for the word Nabisco. Although the use of Nabisco began to be associated with the National Biscuit Company early in its history, it was not until this date that the company began to use the Nabisco name with regularity. Post-war expansion was huge for Nabisco as international markets opened in the wake of the Second World War.[8]

In the fifties, growth within the company continued unabated as did research. Most of the bakeries in use by Nabisco today were opened during this era. In 1952, the triangular shield and its corner placement on the package were adopted. Today it is associated with all Nabisco products and advertisements. [9]

In the sixties diversification continued and Nabisco expanded into the Japanese sector in the seventies. The merger between Standard Brands and Nabisco in the tightening market of the eighties was a natural and needed step to respond to new needs. The R.J.R., Nabisco, Standard Brands merger and the infighting for profit, so accurately depicted in the book and movie "Barbarians at the Gate," does not seem to have weakened the line. This struggle seems to have helped the company to focus on who it is and what it does. Hopefully Nabisco and its products will continue their long and successful run into the new century. Nabisco and the Nabisco Trademarks are registered by the respective companies, where applicable trademarks and slogans are licensed, protected, and the sole property of the companies.

New York Biscuit Company
New York, N.Y.
Formed 1890

New York Biscuit brought twenty-three bakeries to National Biscuit in ten states concentrated in New York and New England.[10]

John Pearson	Newburyport,	Est. 1792
Wholesale Baker	Ms.	
Bent & Co.	Milton, Ms.	Est. 1801
Bent's Handmade		
Water Crackers		
Kennedy Biscuit Works	Boston Ms.	Est. 1805
Kennedy Commons		
Fig Newton — first		
produced 1892 by		
Mitchell's patented		
machine		
Brighton		
Boston Family		
Cambridge Salts		
Beacon Hill		
Shrewsbury		
Melrose		
Plants in Cambridgeport &		
Chicago in 1890		
Binckerhoff and Company		
Butter crackers &		
soda crackers		
Anger Brothers		
Zwieback		
Larrabee Company		
Sweet Biscuit		
Hetfield and Ducker		
Lemon Snaps,		
Claimed invention		
of animal crackers		
Vandeveer and Holmes Biscuit		Est. 1876
Originated the glass front tin		
Claimed invention of		
animal crackers		

Daniel Canty Bakers	
Butter Crackers	
Holmes and Coutts	
Sweet Biscuits &	
Sugar Wafers	
J.D. Gilmore and Company	
Sweet Crackers	
Wilson Biscuit Company	Philadelphia, Pa.
Parks and Savage	Hartford, Co.
J.D. Mason and Company	Baltimore, My.
Burlington Bread Co.	Burlington, Va.
New Haven Baking Co.	New Haven, Co.
Treadwell and Harris	New York, N.Y.

New York Biscuit built the largest bakery in the world in New York City and opened its doors soon after forming in 1890. New York Biscuit's product line brand names included Boston, Harvard, Cambridge Salts, Beacon Hill, Brighton, Shrewsbury, Melrose, The Boston Family, The Mayflower Milk, The Waverly, The Newton, Riverdale, and Bedford. Most of these were adopted from the Kennedy line of Boston. [11]

American Biscuit Company
Chicago, Illinois
Formed 1890

American Biscuit Company brought forty companies in fifteen states to the National Biscuit Company. These companies were concentrated in Iowa, Illinois, and Missouri. [12]

Sommer-Richardson Baking	St. Joseph, MO.
Premium Saltines	
Red Cross Label	
Bremner Bakery	Chicago, IL.
Carpenter and Underwood	Milwaukee, WI.
Dozier Baking Company	St. Louis, MO.
Langeles Bakery	New Orleans, LA.
Kansas City Baking Company	Kansas City, MO.
Loose Brothers Aldridge Bakery	Chicago, IL.
Lillibridge-Bremer Baking	Minneapolis, MN.
Decatur Biscuit Company	Illinois
Hamilton Company	New Jersey

The American Biscuit Company went into production at the heart of the New York Biscuit empire in 1890 when American opened shop in New York City. Sommer was sent to head the operation and his slogan, "Polly want a cracker," followed him.[13]

American Biscuit Company representatives were known as "Polly boys" and were reputed to have been recruited from the toughs of Hell's kitchen. American chose the following as product names to compete with New York Biscuit: Manhattan, Fifth Avenue, Albany Mixed, Jersey Toast, Manhattan Wafer, Iced Manhattan, Manhattan Jelly.[14]

United States Baking Company
Philadelphia Pa.

The United States Baking Company brought thirty-eight bakeries in nine states to National Biscuit Company, bakeries which were concentrated in Ohio, Indiana, Pennsylvania, and Michigan.[15]

The Only Known Member
Marvin Baking Company   Pittsburgh, Pa.

In 1898 the United States Baking Company, The New York Biscuit Company, and the American Biscuit Company joined forces to end the biscuit war and formed the National Biscuit Company. The following companies were absorbed, bought, created, or merged with National Biscuit Company:

Cleveland Bakery & Cracker Co.	Cleveland, Ohio	
Miller Bakery		
Elliott Bakery		
Dale-Care Bakery		
Iten Biscuit Company	Omaha, NB.	1928
National Cracker Co. Affiliated with National Biscuit at its inception	Cedar Rapids, Iowa	
York Pretzel Joined Nabisco	York, Pa.	1925
F.H. Bennett Biscuit Co. Milk Bone Dog Biscuit Joined Nabisco	New York, N.Y.	1931

Other companies involved with snack food production acquired and/or divested by R.J.R./Nabisco/Standard Brands:

Christie, Brown, and Co. Bakeries Joined Nabisco 1928	Canada
Cream of Wheat Founded 1890/ Diamond Milling Joined Nabisco in 1962.	Minnesota
Curtiss Candies Formed 1915-17 by Otto Schnering Joined Standard Brands in 1964, Product lines sold to Nestle.	Chicago, IL.
Holland Rusk Co. Joined in 1928, as a baking interest.	Holland, Michigan
Huntley and Palmer British bakery — began in the 1820 in Reading, England. Palmer joined in 1841 and automated the baking process. Huntley and his son, an iron monger, first created tins to ship biscuits in to keep them fresh. This company was acquired by Nabisco in the early 1980s. Huntley and Palmer had acquired Peek Frean's, Makers of Pearl Biscuit in the twenties. They also controlled Jacob and Co., who manufactured Jacob's Cream Cracker in 1969. Acquired by Nabisco in the 1980s.	England
Life Savers Candy Formed 1912, Lifesavers had already merged with Beech Nut when purchased. Purchased 1981 by Nabisco.	Cleveland, Ohio
National Biscuit Company Formed 1925 as The National Bread Company In 1927, started with seven bakeries in Albany, Syracuse, Buffalo, Cincinnati, Cleveland, Indianapolis, and Pittsburgh. By the end of the year, the National Bread Company had purchased bakeries in Birmingham, Houston, San Antonio, Charleston, Wilmington, and other locations.	Canada
National Milling Company Formed 1927	
Christie, Brown, & Company Ltd. Purchased in 1928	Toronto, Canada
McLaren Consolidated Cones Joined Nabisco in 1928 Ice cream cone production.	Dayton, Ohio
Oxford Biscuit Fabrik Founded late 1920s joined Nabisco 1963	Hjorring Denmark
Planter's Peanuts Formed 1906 Purchased by Standard Brands	Wilkes-Barre Pa.
Shredded Wheat Invented by William Ford and Henry Perky, 1893. The Shredded Wheat "Palace of Light" factory at Niagara was built in 1901.	New York
Triscuit Cracker. Joined Nabisco 1928	
James O. Welch Candies Formed 1927 Joined Nabisco 1963	
Walker's Crisps Acquired by Standard Brands in the early 1980s	England

National Biscuit Company represented nineteen bakeries in New York state, fourteen in Ohio, ten in Pennsylvania, nine in Illinois, eight in Massachusetts, seven in Iowa, seven in Indiana, and seven in Michigan at its inception. A total of one hundred and fourteen bakeries were involved. At the joining of the companies (1898) the following lines were in production:[16]

Philadelphia Bakery
   Oyster Crackers
   Sultanas Social Teas
Milwaukee Bakery
   Bismarcks Animal Crackers
   Ladyfingers Boston
   Butter Crackers
   Newports
Crawford and Zeller   Mansfield, Ohio
   13 varieties of oyster
   crackers Cornhills
   Lemon Biscuits
   Oatmeal Crackers
New York Bakery   Bethune St., NYC
   Bee Hives, Baseballs,
   Alberts, Bridal Veils,
   Manhattan Wafers,
   Vienna Creams,
   Paris Bars

The Nabisco Company states that between inception and 1902 the following crackers and cookies were introduced by Nabisco.

Uneeda	1899
Jinjer Wafer	1899
Zuzu Ginger Snaps	1899
Named for a character in "Forbidden Fruit,"	
a play, by Dion Boucicault.	
Graham Cracker	1899
Invented by Slyvester Graham early 1800,	
produced by many companies.	
Fig Newton Cake	1899
Kennedy Biscuit Works	1892
Premium Saltines	1899
Sommer-Richardson Baking	predate 1876
Snowflake Crackers	
Social Tea Wafer	1899
Holmes and Coutts Tea Biscuit	1889
Oysterette	1901
Kennedy Biscuit Oyster Cracker	1890
Wilson Biscuit Oyster Cracker	1879
Nabisco Sugar Wafers	1901
Came in several flavors and was produced	
by many companies.	
Barnum Animal Crackers	1901
Vandeveer and Holmes Animal Cracker	
Hetfield and Ducker Animal Cracker	
Arrowroot Cracker	
Zwieback Cracker	
Anger's Celebrated Zwieback	1879

Forty-four products were in production by 1908 including the following:[17]

Ginger Snaps	Bonnie Doones
Crown Pilot Crackers	Saratoga Flakes
Baronets	Juniors Melodies
Cameo Cream Sandwiches	Mary Ann's
Oatmeal Cookies	Lemon Snaps
Saltinas	Coconut Dainties
Vanilla Wafers	Chocolate Wafers

Festinos	Five o'clock Tea Biscuits
Cheese Tidbits	

The 1912 additions to the product line included:

Mother Goose Biscuits — biscuit bearing Mother Goose legends.
Veronese Biscuits — early Green name suggestion for the product that became Uneeda Biscuit.
Oreo — origin unknown — possibly from the Greek word, "oreo", meaning mountain and related to the original shape of the cookie. Derived from an earlier product, Bouquet. Variations have been made including a single-cracker Oreo, a vanilla Oreo, and a lemon filled Oreo. Size has also changed.
Lorna Doone — named for a character in the R.D. Blackmore novel.

The 1913 additions to the product line:

Mallormars - derived from an earlier product called "Marshmallow Cream Sandwich." Mallormars were designed for the "In-er-Seal" package but were also shipped in bulk.

Other early (pre-1920) products included:

Lillian Russells	San Juans
Tokens	Butter Thin Biscuit
Lotus	Anola Peanut Sandwich
Hippodromes	

"By 1915, new bakeries had were constructed in Chicago, New York, Houston (1910), and Kansas City (1911), with a total of eleven new bakeries under construction. National Biscuit had at this time a total of fifty-four bakeries, thirty-two owned by the company and twenty-two leased. No town in the nation was more than an overnight trip from a National Biscuit Company bakery."[18]

In 1920, the following products were alive at National Biscuit and doing well:[19]

Uneeda Biscuit	Graham Crackers
Saratoga Flakes	Zuzu Ginger Snaps
Nabisco Sugar Wafers	Tokens
National Arrowroot Biscuit	Coconut Dainties
Butter Thin Biscuits	Cameo Biscuit
Social Tea Biscuit	Fig Newton Cakes
Five o'clock Tea Biscuit	

Other popular products whose names once graced the Nabisco line include:[20]

Unity	Dulcet Amoret
Robena Grahams	Manor
Ponderosa	Velvia
Solara	Mirabel
Sylph	Hobbies
Seminole Gems	Champion
Tangs	Almona Aces
American Pride	Table Grahams
Popularity	Slim Jane
Copia Butteroons	Cubs
Toytown	

In 1923, Log Cabin Brownies and National Biscuit Company Alphabets were being manufactured. The Mickey Mouse cracker was in production in 1937. These products are of interest because of the packaging. Also introduced in the twenties were the Peanut Sandwich Packet and the Sorbetto Sandwich Packet, both forerunners of Nabs, a 1928 addition to the Nabisco line.[21]

Partial list of current product lines (1995) [22]

Barnum's Animals — The animal crackers line was carried by two of the companies that merged in the original Nabisco merger. Barnum Animal Crackers were introduced by Nabisco in 1902. The string allowed the boxes to be used as Christmas tree ornaments.

Nabisco Grahams — discovered by Sylvester Graham in 1829 as a health food, a product line of most biscuit companies a part of the Nabisco line since 1898.

Newtons — created by Kennedy Biscuit Works of Boston, Massachusetts. Production was allowed by Henry Mitchell's unique double funnel machine. This cookie predates Nabisco and this bakery was one of the original units of Nabisco.

Oreo — introduced in 1912. Although the name is a mystery, it is probably the all-time favorite of children and adults.

Premium Saltines — predate the founding of Nabisco, They were the premier product of Sommer-Richardson Baking of St. Joseph, Missouri, under their old Red Cross label.

Ritz — first mass produced in 1934, Ritz quickly became a staple of the Nabisco line.

Chips Ahoy — Nabisco chocolate chip cookie, introduced in 1963.

Lorna Doone — Nabisco's shortbread cookie, It was introduced in 1912 and named for Richard Doddridge Blackmore's novel by the same name whose central theme is the Scottish highlands.

Triscuit — first manufactured by Henry Perky and William Ford in Denver's Porter House using a machine they developed in 1892 for making shredded wheat. Triscuit was an extension of that product.

Nabisco Bulk Packaging and Store Distribution Systems

In 1900, the National Biscuit Company logo looked like this illustration. In 1918, the word Iner-Seal was removed and N.B.C. was placed in each of the three quadrants. The word, UNEEDA was added in the mid-1920s. In 1941, the divider was removed from the circle and replaced with the word, NABISCO. In 1952, the familiar triangular logo was adopted and placed in the corner of all packaging. That logo was modified in both 1958 and 1992 but only slightly.

Wooden Cases

American Biscuit Company, wooden box, with Polly label — $50-$75.

Labels must be excellent on all packing boxes for top value.

American Biscuit Company (Polly Box), circa 1895.

American Biscuit Company (Polly Box), circa 1895.

New York Biscuit Company, wooden box — $50-$75.
United States Baking Company, wooden box — $30-$50.
National Biscuit or other subsidiary bakery, wooden box — $25-$40.

Brass and Glass Bulk Tins

The glass front container in brass or tin was first used by Vandeveer and Holmes in the 1870's. This allowed the consumer to view the product and was considered a great advantage. By the time of the formation of the National Biscuit Company, it was the primary system of delivery. Many merchants preferred the glass jar and its use was widespread by the turn of the century. National Biscuit used both a glass and a tin upper insert with the words National Biscuit company. This was stamped in the brass on some tins. This brass Container was also used by Johnston Bakery in Wisconsin and many other cookie producers. Its use seemed to be preferred in the North and Midwest. Ginger Snaps and the numerical label were glued on the glass and could be removed when the container was recycled by the company. A deposit was required by the merchant.

Nabisco, brass front tin, glass inserts — $60-$90.

Nabisco, brass front tin, Nabisco on tin with glass lower insert, National Biscuit Company on center bar — $45-$75. The glass on glass while more durable as to finish, was frequently broken, thus the premium price.

National Biscuit Brass Front Tin with Two Glass Inserts showing paper labels, 1900-1917.

Second version of the Brass Front Tin with the glass upper insert, 1900-1917.

First version of the Brass Front Tin with the upper tin insert and National Biscuit embossed.

Store Jars

National Biscuit Company, Potbelly jar with correct lid and paper label for top value.

The National Biscuit Company used the "potbelly" jar. It appears with several sizes of type and several types of labels. The later jars incorporate a raised section to accommodate labeling. National Biscuit Company is embossed in the glass. This jar is usually priced in the $60 without lid to $125 range with label.

NBC: Potbelly, 1900-1920. The correct lid is the Standard Potbelly Lid.

Standard Potbelly Lid.

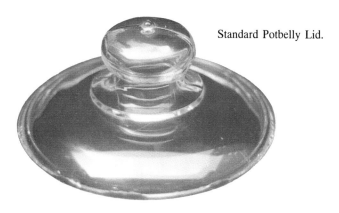

Nabisco Potbelly Jar.

National Biscuit Company, Uneeda Bakery, side-loading jar with correct metal lid and labeling for top value.

This is the second National Biscuit Company jar. The space-saving stacking idea would appear to be the last jar developed. National Biscuit Company, Uneeda Bakers, and theUneeda, N.B.C. emblem are all embossed in the glass. Common asking price is $50- $100.

Standard Nabisco Lid.

NBC: Side Loader, 1923-1941. The correct lid is the Standard Nabisco Lid.

Nabisco Side Loader.

National Biscuit Company, Uneeda Bakery, stacking jar with correct metal lid and labeling for top value — $50-$100.

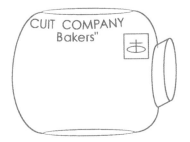

National Biscuit also developed thier version of the space-saving jar. These jars stacked using an interlocking prong molded into the glass. This jar appears to have been developed after World War I when Uneeda was added to the logo. The lettering states National Biscuit Company, Uneeda Bakers. $50-$90.

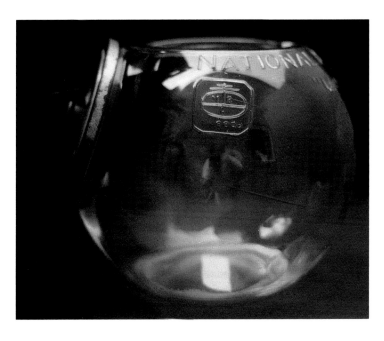

NBC: Stacking Jar, 1923-1941. The correct lid is the Standard Nabisco Lid shown previously.

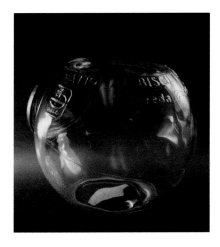

Nabisco Stacking Jar.

Brass Box Fronts

These frames are commonly encountered. Thousands, actually millions, of these were made by many companies for National Biscuit, therefore nearly infinite variations exist. See the production numbers for N.B.C. brass front tins if you don't believe it. Do not assume that if something is not listed here, it is a rare variation, it probably is not. The only real premium at this point is the early closure system. To see someone so foolish as to price a common variant for one hundred dollars in today's market is lunacy. While hoping to part lunatics from their money is a sport as old as man ... most of us are not P.T. Barnum. The same applies to the inserts for the frame. Nabisco has ten thousand in a warehouse somewhere.

Nabisco brass box fronts (early type), National Biscuit Company embossed on center bar with two Nabisco emblems at ends of cross bar, retainers for tin and glass run vertical, sides wrap completely around the box, marked, patented March 23, 1923, Property of National Biscuit Company, "Uneeda Bakers" — $15-$35.

Brass Box Front. The early version with an early insert, 1918-1923.

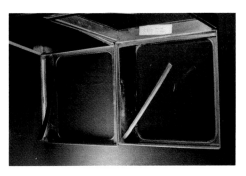

Nabisco Box Front with the early style spring on the right and the later style spring on the left.

Nabisco brass box front, (second type) National Biscuit Company embossed on center bar, without Nabisco emblem, sides wrap completely around the box, second closure system, marked patent applied for — $10-$25.

Nabisco nickel or chrome box front, standard improved retainer for glass, marked Property of National Biscuit Company, patent applied for — $10-$25.

Nickel Box Front, early version with an early insert, 1918-1923.

Nabisco brass box front, standard improved retainer, marked Property of National Biscuit Company, patent applied for — $10-$25.

Nickel Uneeda Bakers Version with Uneeda insert, 1923-1940.

Brass Box Front with the 1941 insert.

Nickel Box Front with the 1941 insert.

If the Nabisco product box is with the box front, $25 to $35 may be added. Certain products have a larger premium.

Inserts for Above:

The 1920 vintage Old N.B.C. emblem, on eight cornered shield, marked, "A Product of National Biscuit Company," green with red emblem and white letters, on tin.

This box front is one of National Biscuit Company's earliest. The National Biscuit Company name is embossed in the brass frame and is flanked by two Nabisco emblems. The first system of glass and logo replacement is much more inclined to break than the improved style. The Nabisco emblem on the green tin plate is the 1918 N.B.C. type. This insert would have been used from about 1918 until 1923.

See photos on page 95, top and bottom right.

The 1923 vintage Old N.B.C. emblem, on eight cornered shield, with Uneeda underneath, "Uneeda Bakers," in large white letters on light green and dark green background on tin.

Nickel-plated frames were also used by Nabisco. This particular frame is the improved system that has been modified to the simple spring system. The logo is the 1923 type and the "Uneeda Bakers" is also of that era. Nabisco pioneered the use of boxes just before the First World War. By the 1920s, the hinged box front was Nabisco's preferred system of distribution. The fronts were used by most cookie makers for bulk distribution well into the late 1950s and did not disappear until the 1960s. Nabisco boxes from the early years are among the most difficult items to locate.

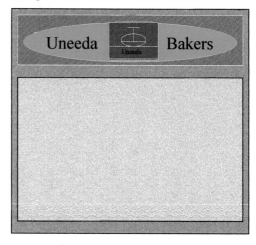

See photo on page 96, top left.

The 1940 vintage Red Nabisco emblem, eight cornered shield, "Baked by Nabisco" with "Trade mark REG. US Pat. Off," underneath Nabisco, "National Biscuit Company," white letters on green background, on paper insert.

This Insert for the "Qu" box frame bears the 1941 logo that incorporates the word, Nabisco, as shown at the right. The final adaptation of box fronts occurred in the mid-1940s. It involved a paper label that could be folded over the tin insert. This served to protect many early tins inserts from damage.

See photos on page 96, center left and bottom left.

Post World War II — Red Nabisco emblem, flat "1940s" emblem on square, "Baked by Nabisco, National Biscuit Company," in white on dark green background on paper insert.

Blank inserts to replace rusted early inserts, post 1940.

This is an early Nabisco box front in chrome or nickel finish. The words, "National Biscuit Company" are flanked by embossed Nabisco emblems and the trademark and patent information is listed on the bottom. The nameplate has been replaced by a Colonial Bakers plate. In this case it was placed over a 1924 Nabisco plate. Colonial was a large Pennsylvania baker and a Southern company from North Carolina. This is probably from the northern company. These box fronts were given to the merchant for a security deposit, much like the early brass front tins. It was common for a salesman from a competitor to offer a better deal and replace the nameplate with the nameplate of his company. The lettering is gold or golden brown on this particular plate. (See Keebler.)

Early Nabisco Box Front with Colonial Bakers insert.

Shelves for the display of these items date from all eras and are usually available in the $75-$200 range depending on your location and the date the unit was produced. Top prices are received for complete units in top condition with early dates. Ad boards are often incomplete or missing and their loss can destroy the value of a beautiful shelf unit.

The origin of the "QU" or "Q" Box

"In 1914, a legal ruling opened the door for the use of fiber containers for general shipping purposes. National Biscuit Company specialists devised a substantial tight container of moisture-proof, grease-proof pulp board. It was put in production at the carton factory in Marseilles, Illinois. It was called the "qu," later shortened to "q" for cube. A brass-bound cover was supplied and each merchant was required to pay a deposit of twenty-five cents per cover. When the "q" was delivered to the store, the merchant would remove the laminated cover and replace it with the new glass cover. The package worked exceptionally well and millions of tin and brass front tin containers were recalled and temporarily stored at Beacon, New York in the N.B.C. box factory. Later they were destroyed. National Biscuit Company wrote off three million dollars with the destruction of about six million tins. By the early twenties the glass front tin was a thing of the past with Nabisco."[23]

"Q" or "qu" box, circa 1925.

Paper labels on "Q" box.

Standard Nabisco Large Circular Tin, 1923-1941.

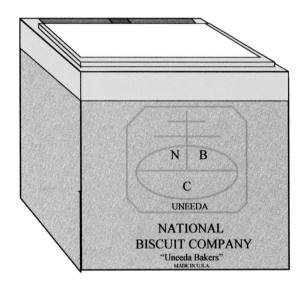

National Biscuit Company box and box front circa 1923-1941. This particular box dates from between 1924 and 1941. It is labeled Premium Soda Crackers. The word trademark appears beneath the N.B.C. emblem and above Uneeda. All lettering is in green on a tan box.

Fruit Cake Tin, 1923-1941.

Child's Purse or Aladdin Tin, 1923-1941.

Assortment Tin, 1918-1924.

Current Ritz Tin.

Circa 1918-1923 logo on a Kennedy Commons advertisement.

The Nabisco logo was adopted with the In-er-Seal package in 1900.

The 1918 revision of the Nabisco emblem.

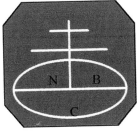

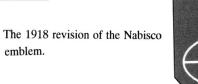

National Biscuit Logo as revised in 1924, included the Uneeda Bakers notation.

This box was used to back a family picture; the box dates from circa 1918-1923.

Ritz advertisement, circa 1935.

This illustrates the last modification of the Nabisco emblem in the square format in 1941. The triangular Nabisco logo was introduced to the left hand corner of all packaging in 1952. That logo was modified in 1958 and again in 1992. Although the dates of logo changes maybe used to arrive at a general date for packaging, a great deal of overlapping occurs, particularly in those years prior to World War II.

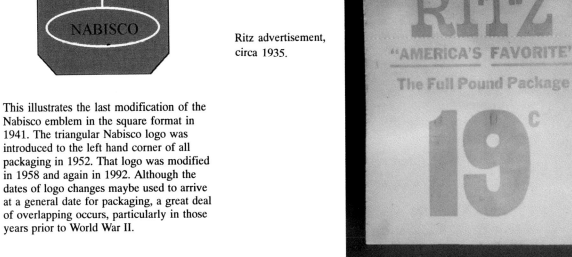

Ritz Store Sign.

Kennedy Commons Sign.

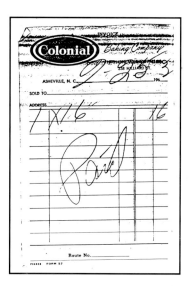

Colonial Bakery receipt, Asheville, North Carolina, circa 1963.

Nabisco receipt showing products, circa 1963.

Nabisco receipt showing products, circa 1962.

Nabisco Endnotes

[1] William Cahn, *Out of the Cracker Barrel, The Nabisco Story From Animal Crackers to ZuZus*, Simon and Schuster, New York, New York, ISBN: 671-20360-6

[2] *Forty-two Million a Day. The Story of Nabisco Brands.* Nabisco Brands, Inc., East Hanover, N.J.

[3] Cahn.

[4] Ibid.

[5] Ibid.

[6] Ibid.

[7] Ibid.

[8] Ibid.

[9] *Forty-two Million a Day.*

[10] Cahn.

[11] Ibid.

[12] Ibid.

[13] Ibid.

[14] Ibid.

[15] Ibid.

[16] Ibid.

[17] Ibid.

[18] Ibid.

[19] Ibid.

[20] Ibid.

[21] Ibid.

[22] Nabisco Product Information Series.

[23] Cahn.

NECCO
New England Confectionery Co. Cambridge, Massachusetts 1901-dates informal beginnings to 1847

Necco, also known as the New England Confectionery Company, traces its earliest roots to Oliver Chase. He invented the first American candy machine, a lozenge cutter in 1847. He formed his company, Chase and Company, in that year. The products he produced are considered the forerunners of Necco Wafers, Canada Mint, Necco Wintergreen, and Spearmint Lozenges.

In 1848 Daniel Fobes also began a candy business in Boston. He produced confections using popcorn and maple sugar. Later the firm introduced jellies, bonbons, and chocolates. In 1865, this institution became Fobes, Hayward and Company.

In 1856, William Wright began to produce candies like those popular in England. He joined Charles Bird to form the firm of Bird, Wright, and Company that later became Wright and Moody. The Wright and Moody trademark "O.K." was found on many of the popular candies of that day.

In 1901 the three companies joined forces to accelerate growth and establish the largest and most important candy firm of the day, New England Confectionery Company. The diverse product lines were rapidly integrated under the new trademark NECCO. NECCO products grew to include "Skybar" and "Bolsters" as well as the products already listed.

In 1933 NECCO strengthened its market position with the acquisition of Lovell and Covel Co., a small New England firm with a highly regarded name in package chocolate. The skills acquired allowed NECCO to produce the "Candy Cupboard Chocolates." The goal was to produce the finest box of chocolates money could buy at a popular take-home price.

In 1961 NECCO acquired another leader in the package chocolate field, The Daggett Chocolate Company. This acquisition added the famous brands of Page and Shaw, Handspun, and Old Homestead to the growing NECCO line. Page and Shaw dates to 1888 when Charles Shaw and Dudley Page began their first candy shop on West Street in Boston. From this small beginning their business grew to become an international name with stores in leading European capitals.

In early 1963, on the verge of bankruptcy, NECCO sold 99% of its capitol stock to the United Industrial Syndicate, Inc. Today, NECCO also produces Conversation Hearts and Motto Hearts, both staples of every child's Valentine experience. The company also markets American Beauty Chocolates. To paraphrase the NECCO Company, "quality is still the same word it was in 1847 and we address quality as issue number one."

From this sound base NECCO heads into a new century bright with expectation. NECCO and "NECCO WAFER" are registered trademarks of the New England Confectionery Company, where applicable, trademarks and slogans are licensed, protected, and the sole property of the companies. Special thanks to Walter J. Marshall, Vice President of Corporate Logistics and Planning, NECCO, for the best history I received from any corporation, large or small. NECCO remembers and preserves the past, something to always be respected.

NECCO Art Deco Jar, probably patterned after the Chrysler building in New York, although I suspect the building used was located in Boston. NECCO dates this jar as being used between 1920 and 1950. However, I would comfortably date it in the thirties when art deco was in vogue. With label and correct Necco lid — $35-$50.

Necco Art Decco Jar.

NECCO Peach Candy
Jar, circa 1955.

Nestle
1867-

In 1866, Henri Nestle formulated an infant formula that led to the production of sweetened condensed milk. Nine years later, Daniel Peter, a neighbor of Nestle, combined chocolate with Nestle's sweetened condensed milk to produce milk chocolate. From this humble foundation the largest food company in the world was built.

The Nestle Company began when Charles Page, an American in Switzerland, planned to market Borden's Canned Condensed Milk in Europe. His plan was not successful. As a result, in 1866 he established the Anglo-Swiss Condensed Milk Company as a limited company in Cham, Switzerland. The name was chosen to target the British and the first expansion of Anglo-Swiss was a factory built in 1872 in Chippenham, England.

Shortly after the death of Page, Anglo-Swiss purchased the English condensed milk company in London and sales quadrupled in four years. Meanwhile in Vevey, Henri Nestle had been selling his newly developed condensed milk as an infant formula.

By 1873, the demands on Nestle by the company were too great and he sold Nestle's to Jules Monnerat. Then Nestle became Farine Lactee Nestle, with Monnerat as chairman.

In 1877, Anglo-Swiss began marketing milk food for babies and cheese products. Nestle launched a condensed milk product of it own. Anglo-Swiss attempted to buy Nestle outright but was told Nestle was not for sale. Anglo-Swiss then turned its attention to the American market and built a plant in Middletown, New York. This divided the attention of Anglo-Swiss between the American and European markets that allowed Nestle to move heavily into the European market.

NECCO Penny Jar, 1930-1950.

Finally, in 1902, Anglo-Swiss sold its American operations to Borden. Nestle continued to export products until 1900 when it entered into production in America. This was followed quickly by the construction of plants in Britain, Germany, and Spain. As Vevey is the center of Swiss chocolate production, Nestle had by this time also developed an interest in chocolate.

Nestle joined with Swiss General Chocolate Company, the maker of the Peter and Kohler brands. Under this agreement Swiss Chocolate concentrated on production and Nestle on world-wide distribution.

In 1905, Nestle and the Anglo-Swiss Condensed Milk Company merged and the Nestle name emerged as the company name, ending the infighting of a decade. Growth continued into World War I. However, the fighting left Nestle in disarray, since most of its production was located in Europe. By 1916, Nestle decided to purchase existing factories in the United States and then Australia. By 1921, Nestle had many factories located all over the world.

In the twenties, Nestle moved to develop new products. It also bought Sarotti A.G., a Berlin based chocolate business, which began to manufacture their products. Although affected very little by the Depression, diversification continued in the 1930s and in 1937 Nestle developed Nescafe, its coffee substitute. Nestea followed in the forties. As a result of World War II, Nestle split its headquarters at Vevey and transferred part of management to Stamford, Connecticut. Dual management continued until 1945.

The post-war era provided excellent markets for Nestle's products and post-war expansion found the company expanding into new markets. Aggressive growth continued in the 1960s,

Lid for a NECCO Penny Jar.

1970s, and 1980s with Nestle acquiring many older products and Nestle, USA acquiring Carnation in 1984.

Expansion continued as Nestle acquired many older candy lines in the United States including a large number of those controlled by Nabisco. Nestle and the Nestle trademarks are registered trademarks of the respective companies, where applicable trademarks and slogans are licensed, protected, and the sole property of the companies.

Nestle Products and the year of acquisition or development:

Nestle Crunch Bar	1938
Nestle Toll House Morsels	1939
Carnation Nonfat Dry Milk	1954
Friskies Dry Cat Food	1958
Canadian Products	1916
Acquired by Carnation	1963
Carnation Instant Breakfast	1964
Nestle $100,000 Dollar Bar	1966
Slender	1966
Buffet Cat Food	1967
Spreadables	1968
Mighty Dog	1973
Chef's Blend	1978
Nestle acquires Ward-Johnson Candy	1983
Bit-o-Honey, Chunky, Raisinets, Oh Henry!, Goobers, Sno-caps	
Nestle Alpine White with Almonds	1984
Nestle acquires Beich Candy	1984
Nestle acquires Carnation	1985
Nestle acquired Rowntree P.L.C.	1989
After Eight Mints and Turtles	
Nestle acquired Curtiss and Pearson	1990
Butterfinger & Baby Ruth from Nabisco.	

Num-Num Pretzel
Cleveland, Ohio

Num-Num Pretzels for two gallon circular, correct color is orange.

Two gallon standard, Anchor-Hocking, Num-Num Pretzels, Property of Num-Num Foods Inc., Cleveland, Ohio, orange lettering. Courtesy of the collection of Ann S. Yarborough.

Num-Num Pretzels: Two Gallon, circa 1955.
Ann S. Yarborough.

Nut House
Cambridge, Mass.

Nut House jars seem to be found primarily in the far West and Northeast. The most common is a standard potbelly jar. When seen for sale, it is usually in the $125 and up range, but anything above $175 is probably too expensive. Go West for a better deal. It is very popular with country store collectors. The jar is fully embossed.

Nut House Potbelly.

Planter's Peanut and Chocolate Company
Suffolk, Virginia, Wilke-Barre, Pennsylvania
1906

The founder of the Planter's Company was a young Italian immigrant, Amedeo Obici. Obici joined an uncle in Scranton, Pennsylvania, where he went to school and worked in the family fruit stand. In 1896 the young man invested $4.50 in a machine to roast peanuts and opened his fruit stand in Wilkes-Barre, Pennsylvania.

In 1906 Obici formed the Planter's Nut and Chocolate Company in partnership with Mario Peruzzi. They chose Planter's as the name of the company because it seemed important and dignified. The new company had two peanut roasters and eight employees. Within a year Planter's was able to move to larger quarters.

Planter's began packaging its product in a glassine bag and pioneered the idea of the nickel lunch. In 1913 the processing plant for raw peanuts was established in Suffolk, Virginia. In 1916 Planter's offered a prize for the best sketch suitable for adoption as a trademark. A Virginia schoolboy submitted the winning drawing and Mr. Peanut was born. The top hat, cane, and monocle were added by a commercial artist.

By 1921 expansion was considered wise and the San Francisco plant was opened. In 1925 a factory was acquired in Toronto, Canada. Shortly afterward the National Peanut Company was formed as a subsidiary and the Planter's principal cities store concept (establishing Planter's retail stores in high visibility locations) spread to many principal U.S. sites. The best known of these stores was the Atlantic City, New Jersey, Boardwalk store. Obici continued to lead Planter's until 1947.

A leader in peanut processing and packaging, Planter's would continue to grow. Acquired by Standard Brands in the mid-1960s, Planter's introduced new types of processed peanuts to accommodate the changing taste of the American buying public.

The earliest known commercial jar Planter's adopted was probably used around 1921. It is commonly identified as the one-gallon pickle jar and is identified only by its label. The label carries the 1918 version of Mr. Peanut and lists the San Francisco location — thus the 1921 date. (Note, this is disputed.)

Planter's was early to recognize the need for uniform, attractive packaging. With the formation of the National Peanut Company and the principal cities concept, Planter's exploded in production of store jars. Two octagon jars were followed by a goldfish bowl in 1929. In the thirties, Planter's produced a variety of jars offering a new idea almost on a yearly basis.

For additional information, the address of the company is Planter's Company, 401 North Main St., Winston-Salem, N.C. 27102. Where applicable trademarks and slogans are licensed, protected, and the sole property of Planter's Inc. Thanks to the Planter's Peanut Pals Club and to Mark Woodson for his pioneering work on Mr. Peanut Collectibles. His open attitude and willingness to share his years of research are unmatched in the publishing community. Also to be thanked are Joyce Spontak and Jan Lindenberger for their beautiful work on Planter's collectibles. Both of these works are gold mines on Planter's packaging.

104

Planter's Jars
The 1921 One Gallon Pickle Jar[1]

Planter's 1921 One Gallon Pickle Jar.

This jar held five pounds of Planter's Pennant Salted Peanuts. The jar is paneled. It has four rope-patterned dividers between the panels, all embossed in the glass. The jar without the label is quite common. It has a baling wire handle with a wooden spool lift. The top is unmarked white tin with a waxed cardboard insert. The label depicts a vintage Mr. Peanut and states in small letters at the top, "With bags and measure." It also states, "Planter's Nut and Chocolate Co., Wilkes-Barre, Pa., Suffolk, Va., and San Francisco, Cal." The lid is a standard screw type, tin with waxed insert, white — $300+ for mint label. Dating of this jar is disputed with some sources stating 1936.[2]

Planter's Pickle Jars. This is the correct lid, white with a waxed insert.

Planter's Pickle Jar, 1921.

Planter's Pickle Jar Label, 1921. Note that the label on this example has been corrected. This handmade correction is common to many of these labels.

The 1926 (Earlier) Octagon Pennant [3]

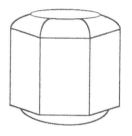

The earlier version of the Octagon Pennant Jar has all eight sides embossed. It stands 10 1/2" high without a lid and 12" high with the lid. The jar measures 7 3/4" across, narrow panel to narrow panel. The four alternating narrow panels of this jar have Mr. Peanut embossed, as he appears on the pennant glassine bags. The front and the back of the jar have two wide panels, approximately 4" wide, with "Planter's" embossed above and extending across the adjacent narrow panels. Also embossed above the Planter's is a large "5 cents," with "pennant" above, "salted" across, and "peanuts" below. The alternate panels are embossed with "Sold only in printed Planter's Red Pennant Bags." The jar has a small bulls-eye mold mark on the bottom. The original lid has an octagon finial rising from a platform lid. The finial measures 1 1/2", flat side to flat side. If the lid had to be replaced, it was replaced with a peanut finial lid. My observation has been that most replacement lids are the lid found on the 1934 square jar. They are unmarked with a scored circle around the peanut finial. Reproductions of this type lid continue to improve. The Octagon Pennant Jar is valued at $100-$250, with the correct lid and mint condition necessary for top value.

The 1926 (Later) Octagon Pennant [4]

One of the eight sides was blanked out to accommodate a label. The jar can be dated no earlier than 1924 due to the Mr.

Peanut found on the label. Woodson quotes a mold change mid-production that added, Made in the U.S.A., to the bottom of the jar, so this jar may appear both with and without Made in the U.S.A. on the bottom.[5] At least two types of labels are found, square and "t" shaped. The correct lid had the octagon finial. Correct lid and mint paper label are necessary for top value — $75-$225. This jar has been duplicated. The replacement lid provided by Planter's was the peanut finial. Great care should be taken when purchasing this jar. Slag glass, poor spacing of letters, and any color but clear are obvious pointers for the buyer. Reproduction of the octagonal finial lid has not been a problem but all peanut finial lids should be viewed carefully.

Planter's Octagon Single Blank Side, Octagon Lid, 1926, later style. The Octagon Lid is correct but replacements such as the unmarked peanut lid below are often seen.

Octagon Finial Lid.

Unmarked Peanut Lid.

This jar is 11 1/2" tall without a lid and measures 9 1/2" across the diameter of the jar. It is 6 3/4" thick at the top and 6 5/8" at the bottom. The pebbly base has "Planter's" embossed on both the front and back panels. The bottom is marked with a blown-in-the-mold bulls-eye mark and "Made in the U.S.A." embossed in a semicircle. The lid was an octagon finial on an octagon platform.

At least three labels are found on this jar, the square, t-shaped, and the rectangular label. The rectangular label is black-bordered gold measuring 9 3/4" x 2 1/8". Large red letters bordered in black spell "Planter's Salted Peanuts." The last line of copy, in solid black letters, reads, "Only genuine when sold in our trademark bag." The large "5 cent" is black bordered in red.[7]

Examples of most types of labeling may be seen in Jan Lindenberger and Joyce Spontak's book, *Planter's Peanut Collectibles*. Variations of this label are known and excellent duplicates of these labels are available. This is the last of the jars commonly seen with the octagon finial lid.

All kinds of lids are found but like the 1926, the peanut finial, unmarked, is most common and the only correct substitute. The correct lid and mint paper label are absolutely necessary for top value. The labels have been duplicated — $50-$150.

Planter's Octagonal Jar with an octagonal finial lid.

The 1929 Large Fishbowl[6]

Planter's Fishbowl, 1929 with a Peanut Lid. The Octagon Lid is correct but replacements such as the unmarked peanut lid above are often seen.

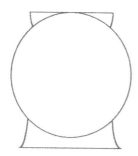

Planter's 1929 Fishbowl.

Planter's Fish Bowl.

Bottom of the Planter's Fish Bowl.

The 1930 Football Jar [8]

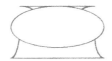

This jar is 6 5/8" high without a lid and measures 8 1/4" across the front and 6 3/4" wide. The oval panels on the front and back measure 7" x 4 1/2". "Planter's" is embossed at the top and "Salted Peanuts" is embossed at the bottom. The football

jar has a pebbly base and a slightly hexagonal shape. The bottom bears a "Made in the U.S.A." mark and a bulls-eye mold mark. The lid had the peanut finial. This jar must have the correct lid for top value — $100-$225.

Planter's Football, 1930. An unmarked peanut lid is believed to be correct but a six-sided jar lid marked "Planter's" on both sides has also been seen.

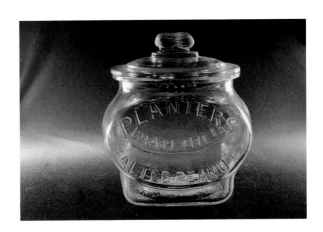

Planter's Football Jar.

Bottom of the Planter's Football Jar.

Unmarked Peanut Lid.

Planter's Four Corner Peanut Jar, 1932-1933. The unmarked peanut lid is correct.

Six-sided Jar Lid.

Planter's Four Corner Peanut Jar.

Planter's Four Corner Peanut Jar.

The 1932-1933 Four Corner Peanut Jar[9]

This jar is 11 3/4" high; "Planter's" is embossed vertically on all four sides between the peanuts on each corner. The base measures 6 7/8" across and has a blown-in-the-mold bulls-eye mark with "Made in the U.S.A." in the bottom. This is considered by many to be the most attractive and original of Planter's jars and consistently brings a higher value. The jar has been duplicated with poor skill and usually involving slag glass. Verification is important if you are not familiar with Planter's jars, but the experienced collector can immediately see the differences in the reproductions offered thus far. It is also important to pay attention to mold marks but the best advice is to know your dealer or work within the framework of the "Peanut Pals Club." This group and its officers have a long standing reputation for honesty. This jar should be mint with correct lid for top value — $150-$300. The correct lid has the peanut finial.

Bottom of the Planter's Four Corner Peanut Jar.

The 1934 Square Jar[10]

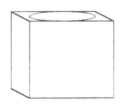

This square jar measures 7 1/8" on each side. The word "Planter's" is embossed in 1 1/4" high pebbly letters at the top of each of the four sides. This jar is found with a light blue and red label and the use of other labels is certainly possible[11] as Planter's tended to use the labels it had on hand. The base has a bulls-eye mold mark with the letters "Made in U.S.A." The correct lid and a mint label are required for top value — $125-$200. The lid has a peanut finial.

Planter's Square Jar, 1934. An unmarked peanut lid is correct.

Planter's Square Jar.

Bottom of the Planter's Square Jar.

The 1935 Barrel Jar [12]

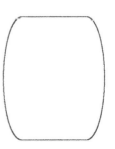

109

The barrel jar is shaped like a barrel. It will be embossed with two Mr. Peanuts, one actively running on both the front and the back. Originally, these figures were painted silver for better visibility.[13] It is made in a two-piece mold with seams on each side. The seams are found in places where staves would be on a barrel. This jar is 10" high without the lid and 12 1/4" high with the lid. At its widest point it is 9" wide. The front of the original has a smooth surface for the reception of a 1 1/2" x 5 3/4" paper label.

The label had a gold background and a black border with red letters bordered in black spelling, "Planter's Salted Peanuts." The back is identical to the front except "Planter's" is embossed in pebbly letters where the label is placed on the front.[14] The base of the barrel measures 7 3/8" across and has "Made in the U.S.A." placed around the bulls-eye mold mark in 1/2" letters. The peanut finial lid measures 8 1/4" across and has "Planter's" embossed across the top of each side in pebbly letters. This lid is larger and will not interchange with other jars. This jar must be correct with a mint label for top value — $100-$250. This jar has been duplicated but reproductions are easily identified at this point. The lack of a correct lid reduces the value of the Barrel Jar to almost nothing.

Planter's Barrel Jar, 1935. The Barrel Jar Lid is correct and the only one that will fit. *Ann S. Yarborough.*

Lid of the Planter's Barrel Jar.

Embossed side of the Planter's Peanut Barrel Jar.

Label side of the Planter's Peanut Barrel Jar.

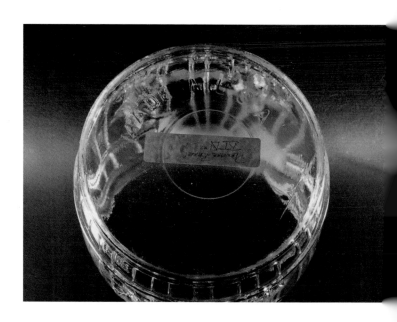

Bottom of the Planter's Barrel Jar.

The 1936 Six Sided Jar[15]

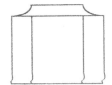

This jar stands 7 1/4" high without the lid and each of the six panels is approximately 4" x 6". The base measures 8" vertex to vertex. The panels are alternately Mr. Peanut and "Planter's" fired on the glass surface in yellow. White examples are often cited as variations, but this is doubtful as fired-on labels of any type tend to fade to white. Yellow in particular is given to sun fading as are some particular jars. Ramon's and Rawl's jars seem to have this habit. Usefulness to the collector depends entirely on individual taste. Any odd white logo jar should be viewed with suspicion as these are sometimes seen labeled as "rare" variations when they are simply faded.

The lid carries the peanut finial with Planter's in embossed letters on each side of the finial. Very common with a replacement or no lid. This jar must have the correct lid for top value — $50-$150.

Planter's Six-sided Jar, 1936. The six-sided jar lid is correct but the unmarked peanut lid is also seen.

The Streamline, The Clipper, The Leap Year, and Nickel Jars

These jars — the streamline, the clipper, the leap year, and nickel jars — have a number of variations. The correct lid and correct labels come in a wide variety of styles and types and must be in place or with the jar for top value. Both the elephant and pretty lady jumbo block labels are found on or with these jars, as well as the square Mr. Peanut label used on the large fishbowl and the ugly kid logo associated with the jumbo block.[16] In addition, a fused-on label and a decal are associated with these jars.[17] Excellent coverage of labeling may be found in Jan Lindenberger and Joyce Spontak's book, *Planter's Peanut Collectibles*, which features Ms Spontak's Planter's collection. This collection is certainly one of the most complete. This book shows the extremely rare pedestal jar that can be identified as Planter's only by the box. The pedestal jars are occasionally seen, the box rarely.

The 1937 Streamline[18]

This jar appears to lean forward. It has a bulls-eye mold mark and a streamlined "Made in the U.S.A." on the base. "Planter's" is embossed in pebbly letters across the front. A number of labeling variations exist and include the commonly seen yellow fired-on letters covered below — $35-$125. Yellow, green, white, and black tin lid is the proper cover. Reproductions or fantasy lids exist that are not confirmed in published works.

Planter's Streamline Lid.

Planter's Streamline without yellow letters, 1937. The Streamline Series Lid and the Planter's Streamline Lid are the correct lids.

Marking on the bottom of the Streamline Jar.

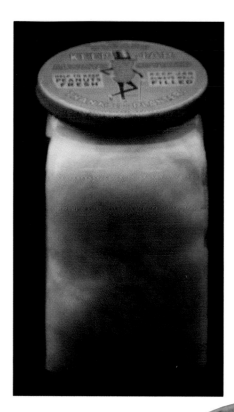

Planter's Streamline, 1937. *Ann S. Yarborough.*

The 1937 Streamline Yellow Fired-On Letters[19]

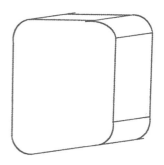

This jar is identical to the streamline except it has "Planter's" and peanuts fused or fired-on in yellow letters across the back. Yellow, green, white, and black tin lid with Mr. Peanut is the proper cover. Paper labels need to be intact for top value — $35-$125.

Lid for the Streamline Jar. *Ann S. Yarborough.*

The 1938 Clipper Jar[20]

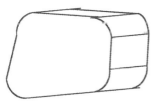

Planter's Streamline with yellow letters. *Ann S. Yarborough.*

This jar is molded in three parts. The upper portion is molded in two parts with seams at opposite corners. The third or lower part gives the jar its slant. It is the short jar of the Planter's jars of this type. "Planter's" is embossed in pebbly letters diagonally across the shorter front of the jar. The back of the jar is smooth and plain. Transfer decals are seen placed on the shoulder or the back and on both sides. These blue-yellow-white decals on the Clipper Jar have Mr. Peanut with Planter's 5 cent peanuts on the back and Mr. Peanut with Planter's Salted Peanuts on both sides. The base has "Pat Appld For" and a bullseye mold mark with clipper 11 jar and "Made in U.S.A." in three lines beneath — $35-$125. The clipper lid is tin and paper labels need to be intact for top value.

Planter's Clipper, 1938. The Planter's Streamline Lid is the correct lid.

Streamline Series Lid.

Marking on the bottom of the Planter's Clipper Jar.

The 1940 Leap Year Jar [21]

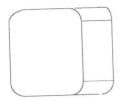

The leap year jar is a rectangular jar and does not lean forward as does the clipper or streamline. This jar has "Planter's" embossed diagonally across the front in pebbly letters with discernible dots at the end of the letters. The bottom has a bulls-eye mold mark and is embossed "1940 leap year jar" below the "Made in U.S.A."

Nickel Peanut Jar [22]

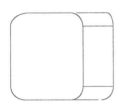

This jar is found with a fused or fired-on label featuring Mr. Peanut and is sometimes called the nickel peanut jar. Two lids are found on this jar. The standard green/yellow and a red lid. The jar takes the same tin lid as the other small square jars, sort of, as not all of these lids are interchangeable. Some sources indicate that manufacture, production, and filling of this jar was interrupted by World War II, thus the lack of uniformity. These jars do not usually carry the leap year markings on the bottom. Therefore they constitute as least two mold variations — $35-$125.

Planter's Nickel Peanut (rear view), also found with a red lid, 1945.

Planter's Nickel Peanut (front view), also found with a red lid, 1945. Marked "Made In U.S.A." on the base.

Marking on the bottom of the Planter's Nickel Jar.

The 1959 Standard
Anchor-Hocking[23]

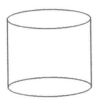

Red on white, frosted, reverse decorations on the standard small (1 gallon) Anchor-Hocking jar. Planter's, with the copy "Salted Peanuts, Peanut Candy, Jumbo Blocks, Peanut Butter, Cracker Sandwiches, Always keep this jar filled with Planter's."[24] Mr. Peanut is the early version associated with the forties. Pricing on this jar varies and this variation is much less common than the jar listed below. It is thought this is an earlier version of the below jar and may be the mystery jar (1959) Mark Woodson's speaks of in his publication — $75-$100.

The 1963 Standard
Anchor-Hocking

Red on white, frosted, reverse decorations of the standard small (1 gallon) Anchor-Hocking jar. Planter's in reverse lettering with the copy "Mr. Peanut" on Mr. Peanut's top hat. Also listed on the jar, "Salted Peanuts, Jumbo Blocks, Peanut Butter Sandwiches, Always keep this jar filled with Planter's." Pricing on this jar varies widely[25] — $45-$75. Photos Courtesy of Ann S. Yarborough.

Planter's Frosted Logo, New Style Mr. Peanut. *Ann S. Yarborough.*

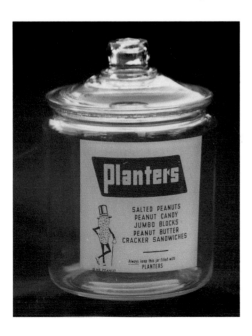

Planter's Frosted Logo, Old Style Mr. Peanut. *Ann S. Yarborough.*

Planter's Frosted Logo (comparison shot). Notice that the number of lines of print and styles of Mr. Peanut are different. *Ann S. Yarborough.*

The 1966 Standard Anchor-Hocking [26]

This jar is described as having a 4-screen decoration in blue, red, yellow, and white on the standard small (1 gallon) Anchor-Hocking jar. Mr. Peanut is displayed to the right of the Planter's logo and the area covered is both large and colorful. The latest Planter's material by Joyce Spontak indicates that the words "Mr. Peanut" in blue indicate a reproduction.[27] $45-$75.

Planter's Jar, 1966.

Planter's Lids

Planter's replacement lids before World War II were usually unmarked peanut finial lids as found on the 1934 square jar. I wish everyone luck in the search for correct original lids and in establishing methods to determine those lids that are from the current generation of duplicates. So far the keen eye can detect subtle differences, we hope, but if we could not, how would we know ...

Pickle Jar with handle and green label — white screw on cap with waxed insert, uniform labeling. [28]

Octagon Pennant Jar (All sides embossed) — octagon finial lid, replaced by Planter's with unmarked peanut finial lid, standard lid size. [29]

Octagon Pennant Jar (Single side blank) — octagon finial lid, replaced by Planter's with unmarked peanut finial lid, standard lid size, square and t-shaped labels were used.

Fish Bowl Peanut Jar - Both the Octagon and the unmarked peanut finial lid appears to have been used by Planter's. The unmarked peanut finial lid may have been used to replace broken lids. Labels used with this jar include the square, t-shaped, and rectangular. [30]

Small Fish Bowl — a paper label with a gold tin lid. [31]

Four Corner Peanut Jar — unmarked peanut finial lid, standard lid size. [32]

Football Jar — unmarked peanut finial lid, standard lid size.[33]

Square Jar — unmarked peanut finial lid, is seen with the square label and a light blue label. [34]

Barrel Jar — oversize 9" lid marked Planter's, has a red and black label that is standard to it. [35]

Six-sided Jar — standard Peanut finial lid marked Planter's.[36]

Streamline — square label, elephant label, the kid that looks like me label, the girl who does not look like she would go out with the kid who looks like me label, "known as the pretty girl label."[37]

Clipper — used the green, white, yellow, and black tin lid, a variation of the pretty girl label or the Mr. Peanut decal in yellow and blue.[38]

Leap Year — used the green, white, yellow, and black tin lid.[39]

Nickel or Straight Jar — red lid or lid as above, this jar is usually seen with a Planter's decal; blue, gold and red Mr. Peanut decal. [40]

Anchor-Hocking Jars — all have a standard one gallon Anchor-Hocking lid.[41]

The four types of Planter's glass lids used prior to World War II.

Planter's Tins

Planter's five pound blue pennant tins are the most commonly found early Planter's tins. The earliest carry the Planter's Nut and Chocolate Lamplight Logo and are marked Wilkes-Barre, Pennsylvania, only. Mr. Peanut replaces the Planter's Nut and Chocolate Logo around the First World War (1916). The move to Suffolk, Virginia, came in the year 1913. The San Francisco addition was in the early twenties (1921) and Toronto was added in 1924-1925.[42]

Planter's tins abound and are quite collectible. Particularly desirable are the early peanut butter tins. For a detailed description of Planter's Peanut Butter and other tins, see Mark Woodson's or Joyce Spontak's works on Planter's collectibles.

The common 5 pound blue tins range in value from $35 to $125 depending on condition, date, and demand. Mr. Woodson provides detailed information for dating the earlier tins according to the lid in his book so the presence of a legible lid is extremely important.

Lids on the blue tin are most often found lettered as follows: "Atmospheric moisture affects peanuts. Please keep the cover tightly closed. Pennant brand whole salted peanuts are evenly roasted and retain their true flavor prepared not in the ordinary way but on scientific principle by experts, best in the world."

Unusual Planter's tins such as the 10 lb. salted in the shell tin always carry a premium value.[43] Early tins had a top that fit over the outside of the canister. Planter's also manufactured a wide variety of peanut products including oils, peanut butter, and other candies that were distributed in tin. Planter's wooden packing cases are also covered in the listed works.[44]

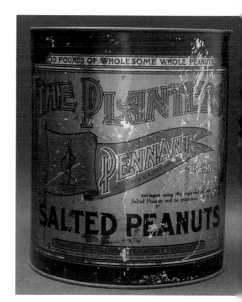

Tin Mr. Peanut Logo.

Top of Tin.

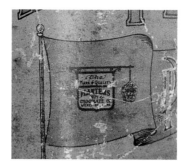

Tin Early Lamplight Logo.

Tin Early Lamplight Logo.

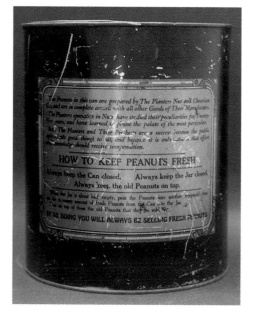

Rear of Tin.

Tin Mr. Peanut Logo.

116

Planter's Cocktail
Peanuts, 1940s.

Late 1940s to early
1950s Planter's
Spanish Peanut.

Senor Peanut.

Candy Tin, 1950s.

Planter's Endnotes

[1] Mark Woodson, *A Guide to Planter's Peanut Collectibles,* published by Mark Woodson.

[2] Jan Lindenberger and Joyce Spontak, *Planter's Peanut Collectibles, 1906-1961. A Handbook and Price Guide.* Schiffer Publishing, Atglen, PA. ISBN: 0-88740-792-7

[3] Woodson.
[4] Ibid.
[5] Ibid.
[6] Ibid.
[7] Ibid.
[8] Ibid.
[9] Ibid.
[10] Ibid.
[11] Lindenberger and Spontak.
[12] Woodson.
[13] Ibid.
[14] Lindenberger and Spontak.
[15] Woodson.
[16] Lindenberger and Spontak.
[17] Ibid.
[18] Woodson.
[19] Ibid.
[20] Ibid.
[21] Ibid.
[22] Ibid.
[23] Woodson. The interpretation of Woodson's research is the authors.
[24] Lindenberger and Spontak.
[25] Woodson.
[26] Ibid.
[27] Lindenberger and Spontak.
[28] Woodson, Lindenberger and Spontak.
[29] Ibid.
[30] Ibid.
[31] Ibid.
[32] Ibid.
[33] Ibid.
[34] Ibid.
[35] Ibid.
[36] Ibid.
[37] Ibid.
[38] Ibid.
[39] Ibid.
[40] Ibid.
[41] Ibid.
[42] Ibid.
[43] Ibid.
[44] Ibid.

Plezall Cookie Company
Suffolk, Virginia ?

Bottom of two gallon circular, Plezall Cookie Company.

Two gallon standard jar embossed in the bottom, Plezall Cookie Co., paper Planter's label, an unusual combination that could indicate anything or nothing — $15 - $25, unless the Planter's label is real and can be confirmed.

Plezall bottom.

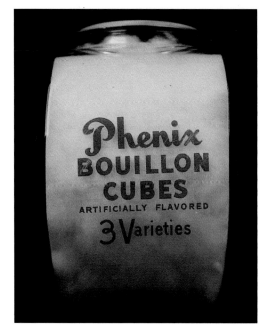

Phenix Bouillon Cubes Side Loader, circa 1955.

Planter's Label attached to Plezall Jar.

Quik Snak

Phenix Bouillon Cubes

Quik Snak two gallon circular.

Phenix Bouillon Cubes, correct color is orange.

Phenix Bouillon Cubes, standard Anchor-Hocking side loader, orange printing — $35-$45.

Quik Snak was probably located in Western North Carolina or the upper part of South Carolina. The jars are frequently found in the Greenville, South Carolina and Asheville, North Carolina area. No additional information is available at this time.

Red logo, two rows of diamonds that circle part of the center of the jar, with a large diamond in center, "Quik Snak" in a large diamond, standard two gallon, Anchor-Hocking style — $35-$60.

Quik Snak, Two Gallon, circa 1955.

Ramon's Medicine
Brown Manufacturing Co.
Le Roy, New York

Jars were not limited to the distribution of cookies and food items. Ramon's Medicines, an old line of home remedies, used them for a number of years. Ramon's used a wide variety of advertising from almanacs to thermometers.

The jars shown featured "The Little Doctor," Ramon's pitch man and symbol. Ramon's was primarily a northeastern product, but jars turn up in Georgia and Virginia with some regularity. All of the standard jars probably date no earlier than the late thirties and were used primarily in the forties and fifties, but many collectors feel they are much older. Until additional information is brought to light, this writer feels the more conservative date is the best guess (1940-1955). All of this not withstanding, these jars do appear to bring a premium when compared to other distribution jars.

Ramon's medicines

Ramon's used many jars; a standard apothecary jar as well as an embossed cylindrical jar are known.

Comparison of Ramon's Little Doctor's suitcase on two different one gallon circular jars.

Standard one gallon with the Little Doctor in yellow. A green tin lid is also reported with this jar as well as the standard yellow and blue tin lid. This jar will often fade to white with exposure to the sun — $65-$125.

R-D Products

Ask for

PRODUCTS

Logo from R-D Products standard side-loader.

Standard side loader, red fired-on label, "Ask for R-D Products" — $25-$40.

R-D Side Loader, circa 1955.

Ramon's Yellow One Gallon, circa 1935-1945.

Ramon's White (faded from yellow), circa 1935-1945.

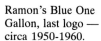

Ramon's Blue One Gallon, last logo — circa 1950-1960.

Ramon's Tin Lid, circa 1935-1960.

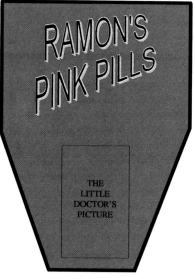

Hot transfer label for Ramon's one-half gallon tobacco jar.

Small, standard tobacco jar size with the little doctor in black and white on a red background; in white letters at the top is found the words, "Ramon's pills." The transfer is very difficult to read but may read "Ramon's Kidney Pills." This jar has a glass lid and a very attractive and colorful logo in red, white, and black. This logo, like the yellow, appears to suffer from exposure to the sun and heat. However, this logo is a transfer as opposed to a fired-on logo — $50-$90.

RAMON'S QUALITY MEDICINE

Blue fired-on label for Ramon's last one gallon standard.

Standard one gallon with the little doctor and logo in blue. Yellow and blue tin lid featuring the little doctor — $50-$110.

Ramon's Transfer Label, One Half Gallon. See separate photo for lid. Circa 1920-1930.

Ramon's Glass Lid for Ramon's Transfer Label, One Half Gallon.

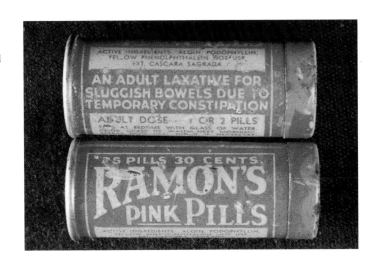

Ramon's Little Pink Pills Tin.

A jar like this was used in the Hendrix General Store in Blair, South Carolina. Today the store is Country Store Antiques. If you should find yourself on Interstate 26 in South Carolina, the side trip toward Winnsboro on S.C. 34 to visit Hendrix Store in Blair is well worth the time. This store is the most like the stores of my childhood of any I have ever visited. There are still a few wonderful places at the end of the road.

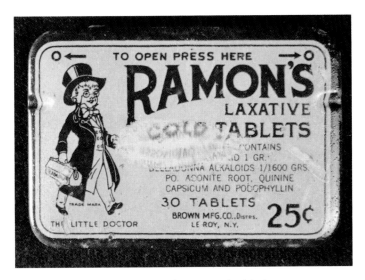

Ramon's Cold Tablets, large size, tin box.

Ramon's Little Pink Pills Tin.

Rawl's Foods
Winston-Salem, N.C.
1946 - 1952

Rawls' was established in 1946 in Winston-Salem by Eden T. Rawls. It functioned as a business entity until 1952. The secretary-treasurer of the company was Mrs. Lillian H. Rawls. Mr. and Mrs. Rawl's had two children, Joseph and Ruth. The business was located from 2218 to 2228 North Liberty Street in Winston-Salem. Rawl's jars are seen in North and South Carolina as well as Virginia and Tennessee.

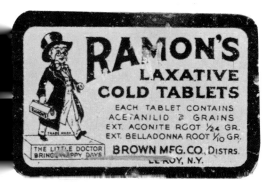

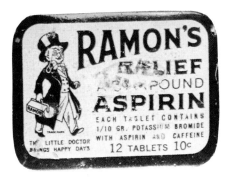

Ramon's Cold Tablets, small size, tin box; Ramon's Aspirin, small sized box.

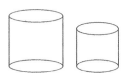

Rawl's Foods logo as seen on both the one and two gallon jars.

121

Red letters, "Rawl's Delicious Foods, Winston-Salem," standard small cylinder — $25-$50.

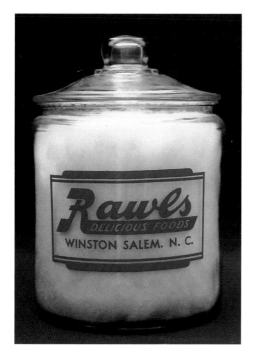

Rawl's: One Gallon, 1945-1952.

Richmond Baking Company
Richmond, Virginia

RICHMOND BAKING COMPANY

Richmond Baking Company box front.

Red letters, "Rawl's Delicious Foods, Winston-Salem," standard large cylinder — $35-$60.

Rawl's: Two Gallon, 1945-1952.

Both Rawl's One and Two Gallons.

Richmond Baking Box Front.

Robinson Crusoe Salted Peanuts
Lynchburg, Virginia.

Robinson Crusoe Salted Peanuts

Robinson Crusoe Salted Peanuts logo as found on the one gallon circular jar.

One- gallon standard Anchor-Hocking, red fired-on label, Robinson Crusoe Salted Peanuts — $25-$45.

Southern Biscuit Tin showing the bakery (obverse).

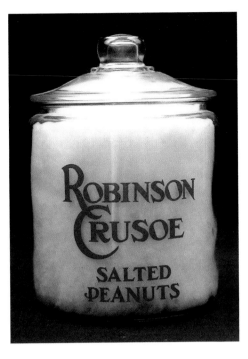

Robinson Crusoe One Gallon, circa 1955.

Paper boxes with a litho cover are also seen for this product.

Southern Biscuit Company
Richmond, Virginia

Southern was a very large company based in Richmond, Virginia. It produced many tins including the F.F.V. line of cookies and crackers. Biscuit boxes indicate that Southern was also very old. Southern jars are reported, as are box fronts. Southern jars reported include one very ornate jar that was used prior to World War II.

Southern Biscuit Boxes marked — $25 -$45.

Southern F.F.V. line tins usually run between $5 and $10.

Southern Biscuit Tin.

Squirrel Nuts
Cambridge, Massachusetts

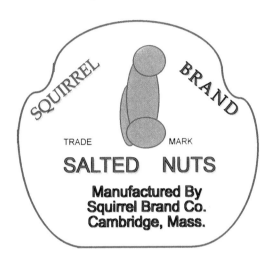

Squirrel Nut logo as embossed on the acorn lid apothacary jar.

Squirrel Nut Ginger Jar or Apothecary — embossed squirrel brand, salted nuts trade mark with "Manufactured by Squirrel Brand Co., Cambridge, Mass." and squirrel logo. This jar was made by the same company as the first Lance Sandwich with the same lid. These are valued from $100-$150. The jar must be uncracked and unchipped for top value. The correct lid should be the acorn lid.

Squirrel Nut Acorn or Ginger Jar with an incorrect lid, 1910-1925. Correct lid is the Acorn Lid for the Ginger or Acorn Jar, 1919. *Ann S. Yarborough.*

123

Acorn Lid for the Ginger or Acorn Jar, 1919.

Squirrel Nut Jar with Label.

Squirrel Nut Square Jar — paper label and marked tin lid — $15-$40.

Squirrel Paper label from the common square jar.

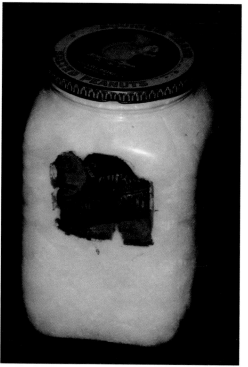

Squirrel Nut Jar with Label. *Ann S. Yarborough.*

Squirrel Nut Lid.

Standard Biscuit Co.
Des Moines, Ia.

First developed by Huntley and Palmer, the tin quickly spread as a method of distribution for crackers. It was little changed until the addition of the glass front.

Standard Square Bulk Distribution Tin without a glass front — $25-$45.

Blue and white logo, "Stewart's Sandwiches, Peanuts, Candy," standard one gallon cylinder — $25-$50.

Standard Biscuit Tin, early 1900s.

Stewart's One Gallon, Stewart Blue Finial, circa 1955.

Stewart's Sandwiches

Stewart's Sandwiches is currently based in Ohio. They manufacture a full line of food products. One pound potato chip tins are frequently seen. The original Stewart's jar lids have a finial painted in Stewart's blue. Stewart's blue fades and wears in an unusual way. The listed jars came from Tennessee.

Blue and white logo, "Stewart's Cookies, Sandwiches, Peanuts, Candy," standard two gallon cylinder — $35-$60.

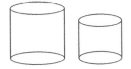

Stewart logo as found on a two gallon jar. The one gallon is slightly different.

Stewart's Two Gallon, Stewart Blue Finial, circa 1955.

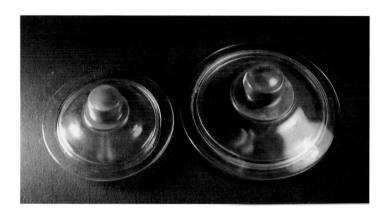

Stewart's One and Two Gallon Lids with Stewart Blue finial.

Stewart one pound potato chip tins — $15-$25.

Stewart's One
Pound Potato Chip
Tin, circa 1955.

Sunshine Biscuit Company
Woodbridge, New Jersey
1902-
Loose-Wiles Biscuit Company, Kansas City
1902-1946

Sunshine was established in 1902 when John A. Wiles, a successful industrialist, and Jacob and Joseph Loose of Kansas City began a baking company in Kansas City. That is the official "Sunshine Story." However, the Loose brothers had just sold Kansas City Biscuit to the National Biscuit Company and some say they had agreed to stay with National Biscuit or stay out of baking. Well, of course, Adolphus Green was not going to let the Loose Brothers run the show, so they left. The knowledge they took with them was used to compete with National Biscuit. Mr. Green of Nabisco never quite forgave them for leaving National Biscuit and forming Sunshine.

The vision of the founders was a company that was bright and modern and produced crackers of the highest quality. They adopted Sunshine as the brand name and eventually the name of Sunshine would eclipse the original name of Loose-Wiles Biscuit Company.

The company grew rapidly. In 1908, a branch was opened in Boston. By 1912, expansion was needed and the company opened the famous "thousand window bakery" in Long Island, New York. This facility remained the largest bakery in the world until 1955. This certainly hit Nabisco where it hurt and is reminiscent of how National Biscuit was formed.

In 1946, the Loose-Wiles company officially changed its name to Sunshine Biscuits and in 1949, opened bakeries in Oakland, California and Columbus Georgia. During the 1960s, Sunshine moved from the Long Island Bakery to a larger facility in New Jersey.

In 1966, Sunshine was acquired by the American Tobacco Company. In 1970, a new bakery opened in Santa Fe, California. In 1991, Sunshine bought General Biscuit Brands, Inc. of Niles, Illinois. Operating as a subsidiary of Sunshine, the new company produces its products under the Salerno and Mama's names.

Sunshine has been unable to furnish more information concerning the companies and products it has absorbed and marketed during the years. Oddly enough, much of Sunshine's history can be found by studying National Biscuit during the Green years ... Old "Dolphus" never forgot the Loose Brothers. Sunshine also owned Gordon's Foods at one time and additional information is located in the Gordon's section.

Sunshine has also controlled the following:

Old Vienna Products, St. Louis, Missouri
Blue Bell Potato Chips, Portland, Oregon
Dickey's Foods, New Orleans Louisiana
Drenk's Foods, Milwaukee, Wisconsin
Fiesta Foods Inc., Phoenix Arizona
W.P. Ihrie and Sons, Baltimore, Maryland
Klein's Foods, Chicago, Illinois
Mann Potato Chip, Washington, D.C.
Schuler's Foods, Rochester, New York
Krun-chee Foods, Detroit, Michigan
Wickham Potato Chip Company, Selbyville, Delaware
Humpty Dumpty Foods of Canada.

Sunshine Tins, Boxes, and Box Fronts

Sunshine biscuit tins vary as to age and value — generally those that mention Loose-Wiles Bakery predate World War II and can be bought in the $10 to $40 range. See Gordon's for other items related to Sunshine.

Krun-chee one pound potato chip tin, circa 1950, prior to Sunshine buy-out — $10-$15.

Krun-chee Potato Chip Tin, circa 1950. Prior to Sunshine buy out.

Sunshine Malt Milk Crackers, circa 1935.

Sunshine Biscuits, English Arrowroot Crackers, A Sunshine Specialty — $15-$40.

Sunshine Cylindrical Tins for various products including Spur Wafers, Chocolate Wafers, Cheez Wafers — $15-$35.

Sunshine Box Front, glass-front marked Sunshine Products, Loose-Wiles Bakery — $15-$25.

Sunshine Arrowroot Tin, circa 1925.

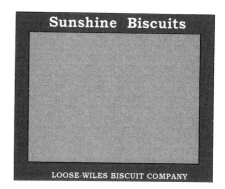

Sunshine Biscuits, Krispy Crackers Biscuits, tin, with paper label — $25-$50.

Sunshine Biscuits, Krispy Crackers, two pound tin, hinged lid, red, white, and blue — $10-$30.

Sunshine Biscuits, Clover Leaf Sugar Wafers, hinged lid — $25-$45.

Sunshine Biscuits, Sunshine Toy Cookies, cardboard with handle and tin lid — $15 -$35.

Sunshine Malt Milk Crackers, as pictured — $25-$35.

The Sunshine Biscuit Box front was never as sturdy as Nabisco's. The narrow frame did not support the weight of the glass or the abuse given by the customers and merchants. Sunshine continued to use the box fronts after many other companies had discontinued them.

Sunshine Box Front, circa 1925-1960.

Sunshine Malt Milk Crackers weight and logo.

Cardboard box pictured here is valued from $5 to $40 depending on the product and condition.

This is the side of a Sunshine Biscuit box from the 1950s. The two Sunshine Bakers flanked the product label that was stamped on each box before shipping. The box front was then mounted on the product by the grocer and it was displayed on the shelf. The box was tan with blue printing. Dixie Vanilla is believed to have originally been a product of the Dixie Bakery in Atlanta, Georgia.

Sunshine Potbelly Jar.

Sunshine Potbelly. Correct lid is identical to Nabisco potbelly, see the photo of the Standard Potbelly Lid. 1910-1935.

Sunshine Box, circa 1960.

Front of the Sunshine Potbelly.

Sunshine offered a wide variety of tins including commemoratives, Currier and Ives, and fruit cake. Tins were and are a major marketing tool for Sunshine and the selection listed is small when compared to what is available. See Gordon's for another Sunshine/Gordon's container of interest.

Sunshine Jars

Sunshine potbelly jar, fully embossed, Sunshine Biscuits on front, Loose-Wiles Biscuit Company on obverse, with correct lid — $75-$150.

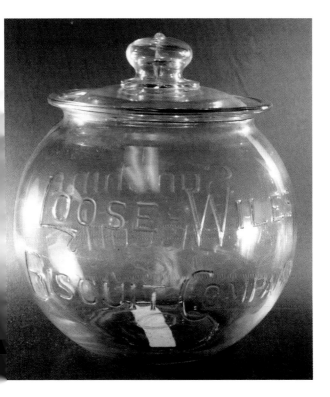

Back of the Sunshine Potbelly.

Standard Potbelly Lid.

Sunshine side-loading jar, lid was attached at collar like the Lance Ball Jar — $60-$100.

Sunshine Side Loader — this jar featured a flip lid like the Lance Basketball Jar.

Sunshine Side Loader, 1915-1940.

Swinson Food Products
S & P Food Products
Charlotte, North Carolina

Swinson was a large producer and supplier of cookie and snack products in the Carolinas. This company was a spin-off from the Lance Company.[1] Swinson's jars turn up throughout the Southeast with a concentration in the Carolinas.

Swinson black logo as seen on the One and Two Gallon Circular Jar and the Side Loader.

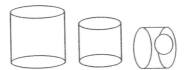

Swinson, S&P (Charlotte, N.C.), black letters, script, "Swinson Food Products, Charlotte, N.C.," standard large cylinder — $35-$55.

Swinson Black Logo: Two Gallon, circa 1950.

Black letters, "Swinson Food Products, Charlotte, N.C.," standard small cylinder — $25-$45.

Swinson orange and blue logo as seen on the One and Two Gallon Circular Jar.

Swinson Black Logo: One Gallon, circa 1950.

Orange "S&P.", blue "Swinson's Food Products, Charlotte, N.C.," standard large — $35-$55.

Swinson Orange and Blue Logo: Two Gallon, circa 1960.

Black letters, "Swinson Food Products, Charlotte, N.C.," standard side- loader — $25-$35.

Swinson Black Logo: Side Loader with Anchor-Hocking marks, circa 1950.

Orange "S&P.", blue "Swinson's Food Products, Charlotte, N.C.," standard small cylinder — $25-$45.

Swinson Black Logo: Side Loader without markings, circa 1950.

Swinson blue logo that is found on the Side Loader.

Swinson Orange and Blue Logo: One Gallon, circa 1960.

Swinson Orange and Blue One and Two Gallons and Blue Side Loader, circa 1960.

Blue letters, "S&P, Swinson's Food Products, Charlotte, N.C." circular from side standard neck attachment — $25-$35.

Swinson Blue Side Loader, circa 1960.

Swinson Black Logo: Two Gallon, Side Loader, One Gallon, circa 1950.

Swinson Endnote

[1] Leon Helms interview.

Taylor Biscuit Company
Durham, North Carolina

Taylor Biscuit was started by a group of men who had learned the snack food business at Lance. They split away with what they felt was a better idea. Eventually successful, Taylor was sold after developing a fairly broad following.

Taylor used a chef, not unlike the Sunshine Chef, as its logo. The parallels between Taylor and Lance and Sunshine and Nabisco are remarkable. Taylor vending machines and boxes can still be found and Taylor also used the plastic containers like Murray and Jack's.

Taylor had both marked glass and marked tin lids and used two distinct jars. One is marked Taylor Biscuit Company and the other is marked Taylor. Both are unique and fully embossed with the Taylor biscuit man embossed to the right of the company name. Taylor jars are usually found in the $35 to $65 range but marked Taylor glass lids demand a slight premium. Special thanks to Leon Helms, who has preserved the Taylor story.

Taylor Biscuit Co.

Early Taylor Biscuit logo as embossed on the Taylor Jar.

"Taylored to Taste"

Taylor Embossed Logo, the correct lid is not shown, circa 1955.

Taylor Biscuit Company, Embossed Logo, circa 1960. The correct lid is not shown.

Taylor Biscuit Company, early jar, circa 1955.

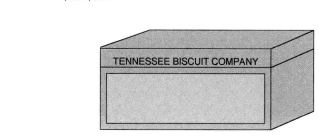

Taylor's later jar, circa 1960.

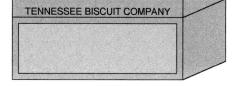

Taylor logo as embossed on the later jar.

Tennessee Biscuit Company
Nashville, Tennessee

Brass front tins with a viewing glass are the most commonly encountered distribution items associated with the Tennessee Biscuit Company (see Keebler). Brass glass front half sized tin — $25-$50.

Tennessee Biscuit Company glass and brass half size tin.

Terry's Potato Chips
Bristol, Tennessee
1932-

Terry's has not replied to my letters soliciting information about their history and containers. However, Terry's was established in 1932 and produced both a composition cracker and potato chip products. They were in direct competition with Moore's in the Tri-Cities area.

Terry's jars are found primarily in East Tennessee and Virginia.

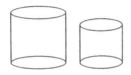

Terry's logo as seen on the One and Two Gallon Circular Jars.

Two gallon standard, red script "Terry's" on a single side — $35-$60.

Terry's Two Gallon, circa 1955.

One gallon standard, red script "Terry's" on a single side — $25-$50.

Two gallon standard with a different logo. Terry's is surrounded by a red star burst to draw attention to the name. Standard two gallon — $35-$60.

Tom's Foods Inc.
Tom Huston Company
Columbus, Georgia
1926

Tom Huston was an inspired young man. He was first an inventor, particularly of peanut processing machinery. Moving from Texas to Columbus, Georgia, to be near the Columbus Iron Works, Tom Huston eventually became a partner in the Medley Manufacturing Company. With a recipe he found for toasting peanuts in coconut oil, Mr. Huston embarked on a new venture. The initial investment was five thousand dollars.[1]

In April of 1925, Tom Huston formed the Tom's Company with three employees. Mr. Huston roasted peanuts in a small frame building in Columbus, Georgia, until early in 1927 when the company moved to the present location at 900 Eighth Street. Mr. Huston soon built the peanut shellers that were to serve the company into the seventies. He also patented a serving package that was a trademark of Tom's Peanuts for a number of years.

The first jars that were used by Tom's appear to be plain small store jars with the distinct Tom's block "T" red handle. The jars are unmarked except for the phrase "Property of Tom Huston Company, Columbus, Ga." embossed in the bottom of the jar. The Depression found Mr. Huston overextended and he left Tom's to pursue other ventures.

Walter Richards became the shepherd of Tom's through the difficult years of the Depression. Tom's continued to expand and eventually recovered from bank ownership in the thirties. In the mid-thirties the block "T" lettering began to appear on the small jar that is found with the, "Eat Tom's Toasted Peanuts, Five Cents," logo. This jar retained the distinct block "T" finial.

The war years were good years for Tom's. The company recovered from the Depression. Although many men were inducted into military service, including Walter Richards, the company continued to prosper and grow. Tom's provided many items for the war effort including food items for "C" rations.

At some point, probably before World War II, Tom's added the sandwich jar to its line. Sandwich jars carried the distinct red finial and block "T" logo. Following the war, Tom's entered a period of great expansion and growth. The black block "T" logo was phased out in the late forties and early fifties and replaced with the black triangular "T" logo on store jars.

Tom's expanded its snack food line in the early sixties to include a wide variety of items produced in Georgia, Tennessee, Texas, California, and Florida. In the sixties, Tom's changed the color of the logo on the jars it used from black to blue. The complex blue logo with the triangular "T" was used until the late seventies and early eighties when the large jar was discontinued and the small red jar currently in use took its place.

Tom's today has over seven hundred distributors and operates over two thousand trucks in a national distribution system. The modern plant occupies thirty-eight acres of industrial property in Columbus. Tom's is unable to furnish additional information concerning logo changes that would date the jars more specifically. However, the dates given can be inferred from *Back Home Where We Belong, The Tom's Food Story.*

Mr. Serff of Tom's also broadly dates these logos as blue in the sixties and seventies, black before that. Tom's may be one of the few companies not to have great diversity in its early jars. It is hoped that more information about the development of the Tom's logo and jars will be revealed as a result of this effort.

Tom's still uses the store jar as part of its distribution system. The red logo, small standard jar was adopted in the eighties. Tom's continues to expand and grow as it faces the challenges of the next century. The company recently embarked on a course of self-ownership and we see a bright future for the Tom's Company of tomorrow. For additional information the address is Tom's Foods Inc., Box 60, Columbus, Georgia 31902.

Where applicable, trademarks and slogans are licensed, protected, and the sole property of Tom's Foods Inc. Thanks to Paul Serff, Senior Vice President, Human Resources/Distribution, Tom's Inc. Much of the information in this article was provided through his assistance.

Tom's embossed bottom, no logo on side, One Gallon, 1925-1935.

Tom's Jars
Late Twenties to Mid-Thirties

Bottom of early Tom's One Gallon Jar. The earliest jars had no fired-on logo.

No lettering on jar, embossed on the bottom, "Property of Tom Huston Company, Columbus, Ga.," small standard cylinder with block "T" red finial — $35-$50.

Mid-Thirties to Late Forties

Black letters, "Eat Tom's Peanut Butter Sandwiches, Five Cents," with block "T," standard large cylinder, red rubber finial, embossed Tom's block "T" — $35-$60.

TOM'S
Eat **TOASTED**   **5¢**
PEANUTS

Tom's Square "T" Nickel Peanut Jar logo.

Tom's embossed bottom, no logo on side, One Gallon, 1925-1935.

Tom's Block T,
Two Gallon with
early rounded glass
finial, 1935-1947.

Tom's embossed
bottom, no logo on
side, One Gallon,
1925-1935.

Black letters, "Eat Tom's Toasted Peanut's 5 Cents," block
"T", standard small cylinder, red rubber finial, embossed Tom's
block "T" — $25-$50.

Early Fifties to Early Sixties

Eat **Tom's PEANUT BUTTER 5¢ SANDWICHES**

Tom's Triangular "T" Nickel Sandwich Jar logo.

Black letters, "Eat Tom's Peanut Butter Sandwiches, Five
Cents," with triangular "T" in Tom's, standard large cylinder,
red rubber finial, embossed Tom's triangular "T" — $35-$60.

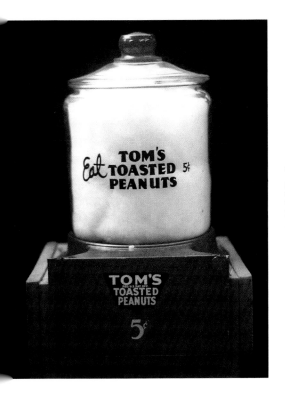

Tom's Block T,
One Gallon with
Block "T" logo and
finial on a counter
display, 1930-
1947.

Tom's Triangular
"T", black logo,
Two Gallon, 1947-
1960.

As above but with "Tom Huston Company, Columbus, Georgia" embossed in the bottom (earliest version) — $45-$75.

Eat Tom's TOASTED PEANUTS 5¢

Tom's Triangular "T" Nickel Peanut Jar logo.

Black letters, "Eat Tom's Toasted Peanut's 5 cents," triangle "T", standard small cylinder, red rubber finial, embossed Tom's triangular "T" — $25-$50.

Tom's Triangular "T", black logo, One Gallon, 1947-1960.

Early Sixties to Late Seventies

Tom's blue Sandwich Jar logo, also found on the standard Side Loader.

Blue letters, "Enjoy Tom's Peanut Butter Sandwiches and Sweet Sandwiches, Prop Tom's Disbt-Not to be sold," standard large cylinder red rubber finial, red rubber embossed Tom's triangular "T" — $35-$60.

Tom's Two Gallon, blue logo, 1960s.

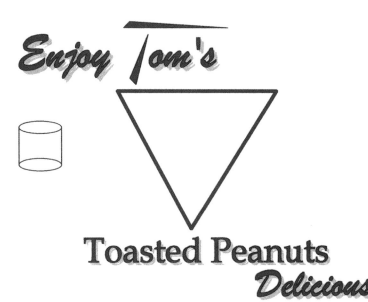

Tom's blue Peanut Jar logo.

Blue letters, "Tom's Toasted Peanut's Delicious, Blue Triangle, Prop Tom's Disbt-Not to be sold," standard small cylinder red rubber finial, embossed Tom's triangular "T" — $25-$50.

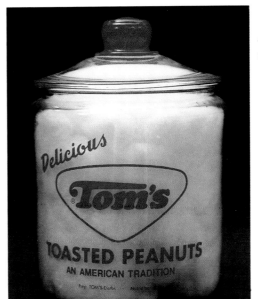

Tom's Red current
One Gallon Jar.

The label below is also found on a side-loader. The value would probably be in the $35 to $65 range. Tom's side loaders do not seem to generate much excitement as most are decals rather than fired-on paint. The exception to this is the Tom's five cents red side loader, which is very difficult to find and has a red fired-on logo. This jar would probably sell for $50 to $90. It is difficult to date this particular jar, but certainly it was in use before 1960.

Tom's Lids

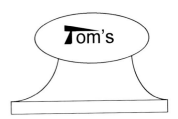

Tom's Triangular "T" finial for a glass lid.

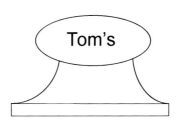

Tom's Square "T" finial for a glass lid.

Tom's early Side Loader, fired-on logo.

Tom's Triangular "T" One Gallon Lid.

Tom's Square "T" One Gallon Lid.

Late Seventies to Present

Red letters, "Tom's Toasted Peanut's, An American Tradition, Prop Tom's Disbt-Not to be sold," standard small cylinder red rubber finial on lid, finial is not embossed, (new) — $25 tops.

Tom's Triangular "T" with standard finial, Two Gallon.

Tom's Square "T" with rounded finial, Two Gallon.

A nickel-plated steel stamping with Tom's Triangular "T" is also seen for both jars. The finial on this jar matches the nickel-plating of the lid. This particular lid originated in Virginia and was on a black triangular "T" jar.

Tom's steel lid.

Two types of glass lids are common with the triangular and block "T" respectively. An early variation of the Square "T" two gallon glass lid with a rounded finial has been noted.

Tom's replacement lids are representative of the free-wheeling nature of an open marketing concept. Many types exist, as do regional variations. These listed were located in the North and South Carolina area as well as in Virginia. Similar lids have been seen in Northern Georgia and Tennessee. Only the rubber/composite lid is unique and it turned up in Greenville, South Carolina.

Tom's replacement lids are found in aluminum and nickel-plated steel. These lids are much more difficult to find than the glass lid. Both size jars have been seen with an aluminum replacement lid that supports a red painted finial and Tom's triangular "T" decals on either side of the finial. These have been seen on both the blue and black triangular "t" jars. These jars were located in North and South Carolina respectively with the one-gallon lid being found in a large Charleston collection.

Tom's One Gallon Steel Replacement Lid.

Tom's aluminum decal lid.

Tom's Two Gallon Aluminum Replacement Lid.

Tom's Steel Two and One Gallon Replacement Lids.

A third replacement lid of lighter construction stamped with the Tom's block "T" on either side of the finial and with a plain finial was seen in Virginia. This lid was for the large jar and on the blue label jar.

Tom's silver composite lid.

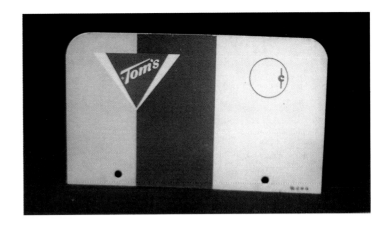

Tom's Clip Sign, circa 1960.

Finally a small Tom's lid of a red rubber composite with the triangle "T" Tom's molded on the finial has been located in South Carolina. Strange Tom's replacement lids oddly seem to increase value but only slightly.

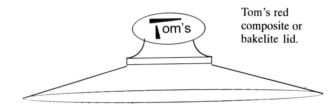

Tom's red composite or bakelite lid.

Tom's One Pound Potato Chip Tin, circa 1955.

Tom's Composite Replacement Lid.

Tom's Three Pound Potato Chip Tin, circa 1955.

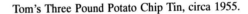

Tom's Coconut Ices Lid.

Tom's Candy Jar
(paper label), circa
1960.

Tom's: marked bottom One Gallon, Two
Gallon, Block "T", One Gallon Block "T".

Tom's: Triangular "T", One Gallon (marked
bottom), Two Gallon, One Gallon.

Tom's: Blue Logo, One Gallon, Two Gallon, Tom's Red Logo One
Gallon.

Bruce E. Naylor
Phone 693-7252 · Route #1
Flat Rock, N. C.
DISTRIBUTOR

TOM'S TOASTED PEANUTS
TOM'S PEANUT BUTTER SANDWICHES & TOM'S CANDIES

Date _2-27-63_ 19____

Sold to _CBS_

	Boxes TOM'S Toasted Peanuts @		
1	Boxes TOM'S P. B. Sandwiches @		65
	" " Peanut Butter Log @		
1	Lifesaver @		65
	@		
1/2	of 10 chips @		45
	@		
	2 box @		7
	@		
	@		182
	@		
	$		

32

Signed _____

Salesman _____

313298-R

Tom's receipt showing products and discussing jars, circa 1963.

MR. MERCHANT!

You can increase your profits through the use of our glass display jars, small showcases and other display units which we furnish at no cost to you.

We consider it a privilege to supply you with this equipment which represents a very large investment to us. Your full cooperation with us in displaying only TOM'S merchandise in this equipment will make it possible for us to continue this service.

a deposit required. They are loaned and always remain the property of the TOM'S Distributor.

THANK YOU FOR YOUR PATRONAGE!

Bruce E. Naylor
Phone 693-7252   Route #1
Flat Rock, N. C.
DISTRIBUTOR

TOM'S TOASTED PEANUTS
TOM'S PEANUT BUTTER SANDWICHES & TOM'S CANDIES

Date 7 — 31 — 63

Sold to

1	Boxes TOM'S Toasted Peanuts @			.65	
3	Boxes TOM'S P. B. Sandwiches @			1.95	
	" " Peanut Butter Log @				
1	"Chip 10¢ @			.90	
1	Chip 5¢ @			.45	
	@				
	@		3.9	5	
	@				
	@				
	@				
	@				

8

Signed
Salesman

313296-R

Tom's Endnote

[1] Sara Crawford and Janis Eberhardt, *Back Home Where We Belong, Tom's Foods Inc., 1925-1990.* Columbus, Productions, Columbus, GA, 1990, no ISBN.

Virginia Baking Company.
Richmond, Virginia

Virginia Baking Company is known primarily through its blue tins. Many of its soda cracker tins with paper labeling seem to have survived — $15-$25.

Virginia Baking Tin, circa 1925.

Virginia Dare Sandwiches
North Carolina

Virginia Dare logo as seen on the standard Side Loader.

Virginia Dare produced a wide variety of products including soft drinks. These were certainly available into the early sixties. Anyone having additional information on this company is urged to share it.

Virginia Dare Side Loader, circa 1950.

Red letters, "Virginia Dare Sandwiches," standard, side loader — $25-$50.

W & S Cough Drops

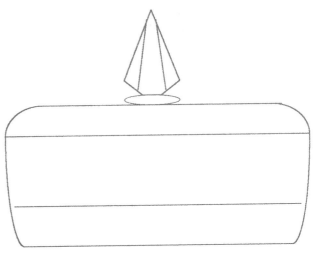

W & S Cough Drop Jar profile.

W & S Cough Drop Jar lid.

Wilhoite's
Washington, D.C.

A very unusual one gallon jar, circular in shape, ribbed with a tin lid that attaches with a wire ring. The logo is embossed on the jar. Courtesy of the collection of Ann S. Yarborough.

Wilhouites, circa 1930. *Ann S. Yarborough.*

We do not copy. We lead
Display of price - Wilhoite's Spec. Co. Inc.
Washington, D.C.
SANDWICHES ONLY

Embossed logo from Wilhoite's upright flip top lid jar.

Williamson Candy Company
Illinois

The little that is known about the Williamson Candy Company must be inferred from the history of it best known product, "Oh, Henry!". Again Nestle has rescued the history of a large company by preserving the history of a single product. "Oh, Henry!" was first produced by Williamson who had a combination retail-wholesale candy store.

The bar is not named for William Sydney Porter who wrote under the pen name of O. Henry. At the Williamson's business a young fellow named Henry would hang around and talk to the girls who worked for Williamson. The girls were always getting Henry to do odd jobs and favors for them, so you could always hear, "Oh, Henry, would you get me this or that?" When it was time to name the newly developed confection, the salesmen commented that all they constantly heard around the store was "Oh, Henry!"... so that's what they called it.

Nestle acquired Ward Johnston Company, makers of "Oh, Henry!", in 1984. Packaging was changed in 1993 to appeal to consumers' preferences for small sized portions. ... Hmm, I wonder, do you?

Oh, Henry! is a registered trademark of the Nestle Company. Where applicable trademarks and slogans are licensed, protected, and the sole property of the companies.

Wise Potato Chip

Top of Wise Potato Chip Decorator One Pound Canister.

Wise Potato Chip is based in Atlanta, Georgia. The Customer Relations and marketing division of that company has failed to respond to a number of requests for information.

Wise Tin, circa 1955.

Wise Decorator Tin with a flower motif and an illustrated lid — $10-$15.

Wrigley Chewing Gum
Chicago, Illinois
1893 -

William Wrigley began his working life as a young salesman for his father in Philadelphia. His father manufactured soap, and as a young boy William would hawk the soap in the streets of Philly. He soon graduated to a horse and wagon and began traveling from town to town calling on merchants. At twenty-nine he found himself with thirty-two dollars selling Wrigley Scouring Soap in Chicago. When the baking powder premium he gave with the soap proved more popular than the soap itself, he started selling baking powder. He began offering chewing gum with the baking powder as a premium and the gum was so popular he decide to market it under his name.

The first two gums he offered were Lotta and Vassar. In 1893, Juicy Fruit was first introduced and the next year Wrigley's Spearmint. Mr. Wrigley was approached about a large merger of chewing gum manufacturers and decided to remain on his own. As a result, there are two giants who dominate the field today.

Wrigley always understood the selling power of premiums and advertising and he used both creatively to maintain growth within the company. Doublemint was added to the mix in 1914 and aggressive marketing continued to ensure the growth of the company.

During World War II, the company faced its greatest challenge. Rationing hurt the ability of Wrigley's to manufacture a top quality product. As a result, the company turned to military production after trying to produce an ersatz gum called Orbit.

In a stroke of genius worthy of his father, a nationwide ad campaign was instituted by his son William Wrigley showing an empty Wrigley's Spearmint Wrapper with the slogan "Remember the Wrapper." By the end of the war when civilian production began it was as if Wrigley's, like the rest of the nation, had simply gone off to do its bit and was now coming home. Though the brands had not been sold in the United States for two years, they quickly regained their popularity.

Growth has continued since 1946 and today Wrigley's products are enjoyed in over one hundred countries all around the world. No mention of the Wrigley family would be complete without mention of the Chicago Cubs and Wrigley Field. Certainly the Wrigley family did much to enrich the culture of the United States in the twentieth century, a long way from peddling soap in the streets of Philadelphia.

Thanks to the Wrigley Company for the information included in this history. All trademarks and slogans are the sole property of the Wm. Wrigley Company.

Wrigley produced many collectible items, like most gum companies, they included racks and glass change dispensers as well as colorful packaging in both paper and cardboard.

Wm. Wrigley Products

Juicy Fruit	1893*
Wrigley's Spearmint	1893
Doublemint	1914
Dulce 16	1927 discontinued in 1975
P.K.	1927 discontinued in 1975
Orbit	1944 to 1949 reintroduced as a product name in 1977
Freedent	1975
Big Red	1976
Hubba Bubba	1979
Big League Chew	1980
Extra	1984
Reeds Candy	1989
Winterfresh	1994
Arrowmint	Canadian Brand
Big G	Kenyan Brand
Big Boy	Philippine Brand

*The date of 1915 provided in correspondence is believed to be incorrect. Wrigley's considers the developer of each brand a matter of proprietary interest so we are unable to credit those individuals further.

Generic Jars

The following jars are generic and were offered to anyone by the glass companies who threw jars. Any logo that is not embossed can be added and decals can certainly be created with relative ease and attached to them. Therefore reproduction, particularly of decals and fired-on logos can happen. It is not yet cost efficient but forewarned is forearmed.

Generic Jar, One Gallon.

Generic Jar, Two Gallon.

Generic Ball Jar or Basketball Jar.

Generic Jar, Barrel.

Generic Jar, Standard Octagon. *Ann S. Yarborough.*

Generic Jar, Acorn or Ginger Jar.

Other Examples of Jars, Tins, and Boxes

Little Debbie One Gallon, Anchor-Hocking, ad give away, circa 1990 — $20.

Chesty Potato Chips Tin, one pound — $10.

Chesty Potato Chips, Terre-Haute, Indiana, circa 1950.

Little Debbie Jar, circa 1990.

Hatch Biscuit Box, circa 1890 — $15-$35.

Hatch Biscuit Box, circa 1890.

Monarch Foods Biscuit Jar, use unknown, embossed lion, circa 1940 — $25.

Pepperidge Farms Stay Fresh Tin, circa 1970 — $10.

Pepperidge Farm Stay Fresh Tin, circa 1965.

Red Bird Candy, display jar, circa 1965 — $15.

Monarch Foods Jar, use unknown.

Red Bird Candy, Piedmont Candy Company, circa 1975.

Bordon's Malted Milk Jar.

Jay's one pound popcorn tin, circa 1955.

Selected Bibliography

Cahn, William, *Out of the Cracker Barrel, The Nabisco™ Story From Animal Crackers to Zuzus*, Simon and Schuster, New York, N.Y., ISBN 671-20360-6.

Crawford, Sara; Eberhardt, Janis; *Back Home Where We Belong, Tom's™ Foods Inc., 1925-1990*, Columbus Productions, Columbus, GA, 1990, No ISBN number recorded.

Klug, Ray, *Antique Advertising Encyclopedia*, L-W Books, Gas City In. ISBN 0-89145-259-1.

Hake, Ted, *Hake's Guide to Advertising Collectibles*, Wallace Homestead Book Company, Radnor, Pa., 1994, ISBN number 0 -87069-645-9.

Lindenberger, Jan; Spontak, Joyce; *Planter's™ Peanut Collectibles, 1906-1961, A Handbook and Price Guide*, Schiffer Publishing, Atglen, Pa., 1995 ISBN number 0-88740-792-7.

Reno, Dawn, *The Confident Collector, Advertising*, Avon Books, New York, N.Y. ISBN 0-380-76884-4.

Woodson, Mark; *Planters Peanut Collectibles*, Privately Published by Mark Woodson.

Pamphlets

The Story of Chewing Gum and the Wm. Wrigley Jr. Company, William Wrigley Company, Chicago, IL.

The Story of Bob' s, Bob' s Candy Company, Albany, Ga.

Chattanooga Bakery History, Chattanooga Bakery, Chattanooga, TN.

Frito-Lay, Fact Sheets and Product History, Frito Lay, Dallas Texas.

History of Hiland Foods and Old Vienna Snacks, Hiland Foods, Des Moines, Iowa.

An Overview of Keebler™ Company, Keebler™ Company, Elmhurst Illinois.

The History of Lance™ Inc., Lance™ Inc., Charlotte, N.C.

The History of Moore's Quality Snack Food, Moore's Inc., Bristol, TN.

Forty-two Million A Day, The Story of Nabisco™ Brands, Nabisco™ Brands, Inc., East Hanover, New Jersey.

The History of Necco, The New England Confectionery Company, Cambridge, Massachusetts .

Nestle Food Company Timeline, Nestle, Glendale, California.

The Story of Chocolate, Nestle, Glendale, California.

The History of Sunshine™ Cookies and Crackers, Sunshine™ Biscuits Inc., Woodbridge, New Jersey.

The Story of Chewing Gum, Warner-Lambert, Morris Plains, New Jersey.

Continental Baking Company History, Continental Baking Company, Public Relations, St. Louis, Missouri.

The History of Hershey, Hershey Foods Corporation, Hershey, Pa.

A Little Encyclopedia of M & M / Mars, Mars Incorporated, Hackettstown, New Jersey, 1995.

M & M™ Mars Colors, Mars Incorporated, Hackettstown, New Jersey, 1995.

Correspondence

October, 1993, Mr. Sam H. Campbell IV, Chattanooga Bakery, Chattanooga, TN.

October, 1993, Sandy Wilder, Customer Response, Hiland Foods, Des Moines, Iowa.

October, 1993, Tommy Ingram, Consumer Affairs, Lance™ Inc., Charlotte, N.C.

October, 1993, Lisa Ohlson, Consumer Relations, Sunshine™ Biscuit, Woodbridge, New Jersey

October, 1993, Paul Serff, Vice President Human Resources and Distribution, Tom's™ Food's Inc.

November, 1993, "Jan", Consumer Affairs Department, Frito-Lay, Inc., Dallas, Texas

February, 1994, Ms. Patti Hoffman, Byrd Cookie Company, Savannah, Ga.

April, 1994, Ms. Bee McCormack, Bob's Candy Company, Albany, Ga.

July, 1994, Greg Perkins, Corporate Archives, Proctor and Gamble Co., Cincinnati, Ohio.

January, 1995, Hugh Mitchum Jr., Mitchum and Tucker Company, Charlotte, N.C.

January, 1995, Jim Arnold, Merchandising Manager, Moore's Quality Snack Foods, Bristol Virginia.

January, 1995, Walter J. Marshall, VP Corporate Logistics and Planning, Necco Inc.

May, 1995, Anne Marie Vela, Consumer Affairs Correspondent, Wm. Wrigley Jr. Company, Chicago, IL.

Interviews

Leon Helms.

Hall Lance.

Ann S. Yarborough.

L. Knighton.

B.C. McWhite.

Index